Praise for *Freedom from Shame*

Freedom from Shame is a brilliant evolution to the ways one can overcome the abuse they endured at the hands of a family member when they were too young to defend against it. This elegant book equally addresses the disgrace of those who once perpetrated the abuse and still hold a secret and pervasive sense of shame for their confusing and violating actions. Its radically restorative message can only be called a revolution, as it brings the bright light of healing and love to a normally taboo and toxic subject.

Leila Reyes does a brilliant job in helping us understand the complicated dynamics that compel someone to abuse their own children. In so doing, anyone who has felt handicapped by the sexual abuse they once suffered as a child or adolescent can gain freedom from the past, and be liberated to live their happiest, healthiest lives.

-Katherine Woodward Thomas
NY Times bestselling author of *Calling in "The One"*
and *Conscious Uncoupling*

If you've been sexually abused, you may wonder if you could ever be happy in life or have healthy, thriving relationships. Leila Reyes's wise and powerful guidance shows you how. In *Freedom from Shame*, you'll find a proven pathway to free yourself from the limitations of abuse, and to empower yourself to live a joy-filled life.

-Marci Shimoff
#1 NY Times bestselling author *Happy for No Reason*
and *Chicken Soup for the Woman's Soul*

In my extensive experience of having conversations with thousands of people across the globe, I've glimpsed the very soul of humanity shining through the most difficult experiences a person can endure. Leila's generosity in sharing her story not only reveals the human capacity to rise above suffering, but she also guides others on a journey of how to transcend the limitations caused by early childhood trauma.

My experience of Leila is a woman who walks her talk and has reclaimed her strength and turned it into love. Leila's book, *Freedom from Shame*, stands out as a beacon of hope for anyone who is ready to move beyond the bonds of suffering and redefine what it means to live a life unburdened by the past. Leila is truly living with freedom from shame.

In *Freedom from Shame*, Leila offers a tried and tested roadmap for breaking free from the chains of shame that have kept so many in a perpetual state of self-doubt and fear. Her candid sharing of personal stories, combined with evidence-based strategies, empowers readers to take bold steps towards a future where freedom is not just an ideal, but a lived reality. This book is an invitation to journey with Leila as she shows you how to let go of shame and step into a life marked by grace, resilience, and an unfettered spirit.

-Lisa Garr
host of *The Aware Show* and author of
Becoming Aware: How to Repattern Your Brain and Revitalize Your Life

Freedom from Shame ignites the reader's journey toward self-liberation. In a world where shame shackles the spirit, Leila guides you through self-doubt and into the brilliance of your true self. This book will equip you with the knowledge and tools to dismantle what has restricted your potential, allowing you to rise with a newfound sense of courage. It teaches that your light is not something to be attained but rather recognized and embraced, for it has always resided within.

Leila applies the application of quantum science principles in the context of personal development underscoring the profound connection between our thoughts, emotions, and the physical reality of what we experience, offering a scientific foundation for the transformative power of belief and intention. *Freedom from Shame* is a portal to a future where you can unapologetically unleash your magnificence upon the world. This is a must-read for anyone on the path to claiming personal freedom from the impact of childhood trauma.

- Dr. Sue Morter
founder of Morter Institute for BioEnergetics
author of *The Energy Codes: The Seven Step System to Awaken Your Spirit,
Heal Your Body, and Live Your Best Life*
creator of The Energy Codes Healing System
host of *The Art of Awakening* Podcast

My admiration of Leila Reyes knows no bounds. Here is a woman who could have easily justified hiding her light from the world but instead chose to use it to courageously lead others out of their darkness. Her groundbreaking book, *Freedom from Shame*, is not only for survivors of early childhood wounding, but for anyone who is ready to free themselves from limitations and say YES! to life.

-Debra Poneman
bestselling author and founder of Yes to Success Seminars

Through the lens of Restorative and Transformative Justice, we see harm as a break down in relationships. *Freedom from Shame* offers survivors and responsible parties a pathway back to their authentic selves and to each other.

In her book, Leila champions the belief that individuals are defined not by their worst experiences but by their capacity to overcome them. Leila skillfully navigates the complex process of taking responsibility, not just as a crucial element in the healing journey for those who have been harmed, but as a step towards personal redemption for those who have caused harm.

One of the book's most compelling strengths lies in its nuanced understanding of healing. Leila acknowledges the individuality of trauma and the personalized paths to recovering, providing a range of strategies that support the quest for wholeness.

Freedom from Shame is more than a guide—it's a lifeline for anyone navigating the turbulent waters of recovery. Leila's expertise, coupled with her compassionate approach, makes this book an indispensable resource for anyone seeking to understand the journey from trauma to triumph. Leila not only educates but empowers, offering a path to healing that is both accessible and transformative and inspiring the reader to envision a future unburdened by shame.

-Rochelle Edwards MS, LMFT
founder of Transformative Justice Institute, 501c(3)

With compassion and insight, Leila offers readers the tools to break free from the limitations of early wounding, allowing them to step into healthy interactions with the opposite sex—and indeed all relationships—with authenticity, understanding, and love.

-John Gray
author of *Men are from Mars, Women are from Venus*

As a therapist for over forty years, I have witnessed the devastating impact of abuse on a person's life. *Freedom from Shame* by Leila Reyes provides a heroic path toward healing. She courageously draws upon her own experience as a survivor as well as her work with victims of abuse and the perpetrators. This book will transform the deepest wounds into gifts of healing. I highly recommend this book.

-Leonard Szymczak
psychotherapist and bestselling co-author of
Power Tools for Men: A Blueprint for Healthy Masculinity

FREEDOM FROM SHAME

Trauma, Forgiveness, and Healing from Sexual Abuse

Leila Reyes, MSW

Copyright © 2024 by Leila Reyes

Freedom from Shame
Trauma, Forgiveness, and Healing from Sexual Abuse

All rights reserved.
No part of this work may be used or reproduced, transmitted, stored, or used in any form or by any means graphic, electronic, or mechanical, including but not limited to photocopying, recording, scanning, digitizing, taping, Web distribution, information networks or information storage and retrieval systems, or in any manner whatsoever without prior written permission from the publisher.
In this world of digital information and rapidly-changing technology, some citations do not provide exact page numbers or credit the original source. We regret any errors, which are a result of the ease with which we consume information.

Excerpt(s) from CONSCIOUS UNCOUPLING: 5 STEPS TO LIVING HAPPILY EVEN AFTER by Katherine Woodward Thomas, MA, MFT, copyright © 2015 by Katherine Woodward Thomas. Used by permission of Harmony Books, an imprint of Random House, a division of Penguin Random House LLC. All rights reserved.

Sr. Editor: Laurie Knight
Editor: Lexi Mohney
Cover Design: Kristina Edstrom

An Imprint for GracePoint Publishing (www.GracePointPublishing.com)

GracePoint Matrix, LLC
624 S. Cascade Ave, Suite 201
Colorado Springs, CO 80903
www.GracePointMatrix.com
Email: Admin@GracePointMatrix.com
SAN # 991-6032

A Library of Congress Control Number has been requested and is pending.

ISBN: (Paperback) 978-1-961347-45-8
eISBN: 978-1-961347-46-5

Books may be purchased for educational, business, or sales promotional use.
For bulk order requests and price schedule contact:
Orders@GracePointPublishing.com

Foreword by Gordon Clay

Like Leila, I have a history of abuse and have utilized my healing to break the chain in my own family. I've since worked with well over a thousand men and women over thirty years facilitating programs such as New Warriors and The California Men's Gathering. I developed Tantrum Yoga® in the early '80s to help people release pent up emotions without resorting to any form of violence.

By 1985 I created and was facilitating several workshops including a four-day residential retreat entitled Healing the Father Wound® for women only and men only, and a six-day residential retreat called Clearing the Air Between Women and Men.

In 1996 I had the opportunity to work with Leila's father, a courageous man who was making conscious choices to openly correct the damage he had done. It was in 2003 that I had the distinct opportunity to meet and work with Leila. I witnessed the work she and her father did to heal their relationship.

It was beautiful to watch Leila build strength and knowledge about the process of healing from sexual trauma. During this time, she was building her professional knowledge as a survivor with a lived experience helping others who had been harmed. She's now expanded her work to include those who have harmed others so she can help people like her father who are willing to step up, take responsibility for what they've done, and make an amends to those they've harmed.

Freedom from Shame offers many benefits. Leila explores the trauma we hold around our family of origin, and how these initial wounds continue to impact our adult lives with the goal to break through the unresolved issues that impede forgiveness and personal freedom. It's written in a way that one can absorb the words while simultaneously working on their own healing through active participation with various interactive experiences.

This book is for you if you're ready to grow beyond the effect abuse has had on your life. You'll discover what currently holds you back and start freeing yourself from patterns, excuses, and behaviors that no longer serve you. You'll examine the story you've told yourself and create a new story you truly want to live by.

The expertise and wisdom in Leila's book will help you work through the trauma stuck in your body. If you're still affected by past feelings toward the person who hurt you and are ready to work through them, if you believe things could be better but you just don't know how to move forward, or if it's been difficult to create truly fulfilling relationships, personally or professionally, this book is for you.

Gordon Clay
creator of Healing the Father Wound®

Dedication

*Though no one can go back
and make a brand-new start,
anyone can start from now
and make a brand-new beginning.
~Carl Bard*

Dedicated to everyone who has the courage to learn how to live beyond the experience of childhood sexual abuse. Sexual abuse survivors are amazing human beings. I humbly include myself among the many who have persevered against the limitation of the meanings made about what happened to us, and is now thriving after unconscionable acts against our innocence.

The sexual abuse survivors I've worked with have shown me the depth of human courage, the value of transparency, and the power of vulnerability. I'm inspired by how fully they've called their lost parts home, and I'm grateful to be part of their journey. Sexual abuse survivors are my heroes. I hope I am theirs.

I also dedicate this book to my father who, like me, is a survivor of childhood sexual abuse. The generosity of my forgiveness pales in comparison to how fully he took responsibility for the harm he caused. I'm grateful for the powerful amends he made to me, to our family, and to our community. Those who have harmed others would do well to follow his example to regain their integrity and honor.

Disclaimer

The information provided in this book is strictly for informational purposes and is not intended as a substitute for advice from your physician or mental health provider. You should not use this information for diagnosis or treatment of any physical or mental health problem.

Content Warning

This book contains topics that some may find disturbing, including incidents of sexual and emotional abuse and rehabilitation of sexual offenders.

Table of Contents

Foreword by Gordon Clay vii
Introduction 1
    Who Is This Book For? 4
    The Gap 6
Part One: Basic Understandings to Guide Transformation 11
    Traditional Therapy and Coaching 14
    Human Development: Models and Identity Formation 18
    Clinical Depression 20
    Getting Help 22
    Trauma and the Nervous System: The Window of Tolerance 23
    Four Stages of Transformation 28
    Experience Biases 38
    A Bucket with Holes 41
    Identifying Abuse 44
    Trapped in Abuse 48
    Identity 50
    Inner Critic: A Bullying Storyteller 55
    Be Your Own Best Friend 58
Part Two: The Impulse to Heal 63
    Your Support System 66
    Identifying Your Growth Edge 70
    Setting an Intention 72
    Aligning with Your Future 78
    Courage 80
    Born Worthy 82
Part Three: Living in The Gap 85
    Barriers to Living in The Gap 88
    Healthy Relationship with Your Feelings 95
    Self-Acceptance 101
    Boundaries 108
    Positive Qualities 116
    False Beliefs 120

Part Four: Repairing Your Relationship with Yourself ... 125
- The Inner Child ... 127
- Listening to the Hurt Part ... 129
- Forgiveness ... 135
- Making Sacred Commitments ... 139

Part Five: Victimization vs. Responsibility ... 147
- Breaking Up with Victimization ... 150
- Tendency for Interpersonal Victimhood ... 156
- Culture of Victimization ... 161
- Child vs. Adult Thinking—Simple vs. Complex ... 167
- Taking Responsibility for Your Relationships ... 170
- Taking Responsibility for What Is Yours ... 173

Part Six: Understanding Sexual Offending ... 175
- Types of Sexual Offenders ... 177
- The Roles We Play ... 179
- Why Children Don't Tell ... 182
- Telling My Children ... 186
- Socialization and the Media ... 196
- Taking a Stand ... 202
- Sexual Offending and Restoration ... 203
- Retributive vs. Restorative Justice ... 210

Part Seven: Living Beyond The Gap ... 215
- Beyond The Gap: My Wound is My Gift ... 216
- Sexuality: Reclaiming All of Yourself ... 221
- Keeping Children Safe: Children's Sexual Behaviors ... 228

Epilogue ... 231

Acknowledgments ... 233

References ... 237

Resources ... 239

About the Author ... 241

The Freedom Project ... 242

Introduction

> *When the whole world is silent,*
> *even one voice becomes powerful.*
> *~Malala Yousafzai*

You're probably reading this book because you're a survivor of childhood sexual abuse or know someone who is. Or perhaps you're the person who sexually abused someone and wants to find a way to take responsibility for what you've done. Either way, you're not alone.

I was a young girl when my father sexually abused me. I trusted my father completely and for years believed what he did to me must have been my fault. The shame of being sexually abused impacted every area of my life, especially how I felt about myself and my value as I grew into a young woman. I've since recovered my self-esteem and my innocence, but it wasn't easy.

In the early eighties I began a rigorous journey challenging the distorted lens of the early interpretations of what happened to me. I believed I was the only one whose father had hurt them in this way. It was my secret, and I kept it well. Shame stole my voice but once I discovered it's our voice that has the power to free us from shame, I started talking.

By sharing the story of how my father and I healed our relationship and created safety in our family, I offer a pathway out of suffering and the promise of a truly vibrant dynamic life with happy, healthy, and safe relationships. Healing isn't a linear process and takes many forms. You can heal regardless of the circumstances surrounding the abuse or who is or isn't included in your healing process. While I chose the path of forgiveness and amends in healing *with* my father, that may not be the right choice for you. If you were harmed, you may not be interested in speaking with the person who hurt you. Or you may choose to heal in private or with the help of a professional to guide you. If the person who caused you harm isn't willing or able to take responsibility and make amends the way my father did, a surrogate can take their place.

While sexual abuse leaves the person harmed feeling like they're all alone, anyone who has been impacted by sexual abuse can be assured they're not alone. Today, it's accepted that one in four girls and one in six boys are sexually abused before the age of eighteen. I believe the numbers are much higher. An expert on sexual abuse asked a group of 500 people to stand if they'd been sexually abused or knew someone who had been. The entire room stood up. The speaker asked everyone to keep standing if the abuse had been reported—only a handful of people remained on their feet. The speaker then asked everyone to stay standing if they knew the person who had caused harm had taken responsibility for what they had done. Only one person remained standing.

While my father's taking responsibility and validating my experience made my life a little easier, I still had to pursue my own healing. The exercises in this book helped me gain freedom from the impact of childhood sexual abuse. I stopped unconsciously reacting to the world around me and created a life I love. Most importantly, I ended the cycle of abuse in my own family.

I wrote this book to help survivors end feeling dominated and overshadowed by the betrayal of childhood sexual abuse. This book is designed to help you gain new insights and perspectives and to update patterns of thinking which may have caused trouble long after the abuse ended. I share resources and stories from my own deeply personal journey and include composite client stories to illustrate commonalities of the human experience as it relates to healing from childhood trauma. I've changed names and details to protect confidentiality.

Reading *Freedom from Shame: Trauma, Forgiveness, and Healing From Sexual Abuse* and doing the exercises will lead to a deeper understanding of the impact childhood sexual abuse has on you and your closest relationships. You'll be able to name and categorize what happened to you from a deeper truth as opposed to any disempowered meaning which often happens with traumatic events. You'll gain an understanding of the tendency toward generalizing sexual offenders and the role society plays in childhood sexual abuse. You'll be able to make a thoughtful choice around whether to include the person who caused you harm in your healing process. Most important, you'll have a greater awareness of what changes are needed to end childhood sexual abuse.

This book will help everyone impacted by childhood sexual abuse to grow beyond the victimization of current problematic family dynamics and become resourceful and expansive in creating the life they want and the healthy relationships that have been difficult to create.

The concepts and resources in this book provide many benefits, including:
- Freedom from the effects of painful childhood experiences.
- Creating a deeply profound and meaningful relationship with yourself.
- Being able to set healthy boundaries and make choices that are right for you.
- An increased ability to surround yourself with emotionally healthy people.
- The capacity to create safety for yourself and the people you love.

Breaking through the limitations of the past takes a willingness to grow and move beyond what has become familiar. Whether you choose to read this book in private or work with a professional coach or therapist, and whether you're at the beginning of your journey or have been on the healing path for some time, I hope you find wisdom here.

This is the right place for you if you've been harmed and:
- You're ready to be free of shame and know what happened wasn't your fault.
- You're scared and are willing to change even if you don't know how.
- You want to access the power of forgiveness for your own benefit.
- You want to learn to deeply connect with others without abandoning yourself.

This is the right place for you if you've caused harm and:
- You feel shame for what you've done and need a safe place to heal.
- You want to take responsibility but are afraid of losing everything.
- You want to make amends and restore your integrity.
- You want to understand what led up to you causing harm to someone you love.
- You want to evolve beyond the impact of the harm you caused.

It's my conviction that all of society benefits when just one person heals. It's my prayer that my healing benefits all who have been harmed by childhood sexual abuse.

All are welcome.

Who Is This Book For?

As my world expands so do my heart and mind. I am willing to stay open and accept all the miracles and abundance the universe has to offer me.
~Kris Carr

I wrote this book directly to the survivors of childhood sexual abuse who want freedom from their painful experiences. If this is you, then use this book as a working guide for your own healing and transformation. Healing is possible when you relate to your childhood from a larger, more inclusive, perspective than you were capable of when the abuse happened. Go at your own pace, completing the exercises in a time frame that doesn't overwhelm you and getting help if you need it. Above all, trust yourself and your process.

I also wrote this book with the intention that people who caused harm will read and gain from it. If this is you, then I hope you find possibility for yourself and a willingness to take ownership of your actions and make amends for what you've done. I know how difficult it was, and how much courage it took for my own father to take responsibility for the harm he caused. It was excruciatingly painful, but true amends helped heal us both.

I recommend that you begin with reading Part Six: Understanding Sexual Offending and take the time to read the article "Families of Sexual Abuse: The Roles Each Member Plays" by Sabrina Trobak. You can find a link to the article in the resources section. The article explains the differences between the three most common reasons for sexually abusing a child. It's important for you to have a working knowledge and understanding of what motivated you to sexually abuse a child. You may find solace in the distinctions, or you may become troubled. Either way, if you want to heal, you must become aware of yourself and why you did what you did so you can engage your own healing process with consciousness. I believe your participation is needed to end childhood sexual abuse, so please join us.

If you're a professional helping people heal from childhood sexual abuse, I hope this book becomes a valuable resource for your clients. I honor and respect your profession, and I'm grateful for the help you give to those of us who are unable to navigate our pain alone. Thank you.

Again, all are welcome.

For the remainder of this book, "you" refers to the survivor of childhood sexual abuse unless otherwise noted.

The Gap

*One can choose to go back toward safety
or forward toward growth.
Growth must be chosen again and again;
fear must be overcome again and again.*
~Abraham Maslow

The Gap is the space between your past and your future in which you reclaim your power by taking responsibility for creating a life beyond the abuse. The purpose of living in The Gap is to turn hope for your future into reality so you can live a healthy life free of the pain and shame of childhood sexual abuse. Living in The Gap is a courageous choice of determination and willingness to explore new ideas and new ways of thinking you haven't yet considered.

It feels like there's a lot to lose in The Gap because there is. However, there's also everything to gain, most importantly your freedom. It's in living in The Gap where you make fundamental changes to become an authentic human being. Living in The Gap, you'll gain a more accurate interpretation of the past and will learn how to relate to whatever happened to you from an empowered perspective. You'll challenge old perspectives and everything you believe about yourself and the world around you. You'll try on new ways of thinking and behaving and collect evidence that the new ways are bringing you the life you desire.

Living in The Gap works because you'll be *doing* things differently than you did in the past. You'll make new conscious choices and take new conscious actions that naturally lead to creating the life you want. In the beginning, change can be slow because of a strong gravitational pull to continue what's familiar—even if it's unhealthy. Making changes can feel like striving, pushing, or grasping to get beyond past wounding. However, as you apply newfound awareness, your transformation is guaranteed.

Feeling insecure and out of your element is a clear indication of being in The Gap. You'll need to stretch outside your comfort zone and stay present to everything you're learning. Your beliefs about yourself and your life will change as you collect evidence of the positive results of the new choices you're making. Your growing consciousness will help you understand you're no longer a wounded child, but rather an adult capable of healing. Paying attention to the results you're getting will help you move away from harmful relational dynamics and start showing up in healthy ways with yourself and others.

As you practice aligning with a deeper truth, you'll gain confidence and strength in your ability to get free of the impact of childhood sexual abuse. You'll bring compassion to the parts of you which need it the most. As you adjust and modify your actions, you'll grow beyond any limitations you've experienced up to this point and you'll start getting the results you're looking for. Guaranteed.

Within each section of this book, you'll find an element called Gap Work. Gap Work is where you'll integrate what you're learning through contemplation, journaling, and experiential exercises.

As a key to liberation, a lot of hard work is done in The Gap. Gap Work is designed to help you engage your learning and transformation through a series of exercises and actions you can take to integrate what you learn. To experience the most benefit from reading *Freedom from Shame*, use the interactive components and do your Gap Work in a journal or in the spaces provided within each section with a willingness to be uncomfortable as you leave old familiar ways of being behind.

Gap Work: Tracking Your Progress

*Progress is not in enhancing what is,
but in advancing toward what will be.*
~Khalil Gibran

Your first Gap Work is to get a journal dedicated to tracking the changes you're making and what's shifting for you. Your dedicated journal doesn't need to be fancy, but make sure it's a journal you'll want to pick up and write in every day. You can do some Gap Work directly in this book on the pages provided; however, I recommend you capture your deeper insights in your journal.

Tracking your progress gives you the opportunity to take stock of your accomplishments and feel good about yourself and the growth you're experiencing. You'll be able to harness the wisdom and celebrate your hard-earned insights. Most importantly, you'll gain access to emotional fuel that will inspire you to continue moving forward.

Keep in mind that The Gap can be uncomfortable. Changing your life requires you to stretch and grow and challenge everything you've known to be true, so give yourself permission to be uncomfortable. Learning how to do your best without beating yourself up for not being perfect is what we're going for. Let yourself be right where you are, and as you just do your best, you'll grow out of the old ways that no longer serve you. You'll raise your awareness, learn something new, and start aligning your actions with the future you want.

Being in The Gap means you're on the evolutionary path to freedom.

The Evolutionary Path

> *Life is a journey up a spiral staircase; as we grow older we cover the ground we have covered before, only higher up; as we look down the winding stair below us we measure our progress by the number of places where we were but no longer are. The journey is both repetitious and progressive; we go both round and upward.*
> ~William Butler Yeats

Navigating The Gap becomes easier when you see you're on a path that continues to grow over time. Life opens up like an ever-expanding spiral in which the vantage point is always changing. No matter how many times a situation or circumstance is repeated, you're never in the same place twice; you're always growing and learning, so your perspective is also always changing.

The process of "becoming" takes time and everything you've experienced is part of your expansion. Because evolution can be slow, it might be difficult to notice changes as they're happening. The more you know what your patterns are, the more quickly you'll be able to consciously make significant changes to start living more freely each day. If you start right where you are, with all the limitations and concerns you have today, then your growth will unfurl organically.

People understand life with greater complexity after they've had many varied experiences. Your past is already filled with a lot of wisdom. Let's take a step by looking at your life from a spiral perspective, so you can see how much your life has already opened up.

Gap Work: Evolutionary Spiral Timeline

> *Your sacred space is where you can find yourself again and again.*
> ~Joseph Campbell

Writing down a timeline of your life in the form of a spiral can help you see the trajectory of your life up to this point. You'll write down significant experiences of your life in chronological order and then you'll look at your life as a whole.

Step 1—Write your timeline. Start from birth and include significant events and experiences you've had. Was there a divorce? A loss? A super happy time? Include what stands out as meaningful to you. Include experiences that are important to your growth and development of the person you are today.

Once you have your timeline, you'll create a visual representation of your life in a spiral.

Step 2—Choose the size of paper big enough to write your spiral timeline. Start in the center with your birth and work clockwise to the outer edges of the paper.

As an example, here's my spiral timeline:

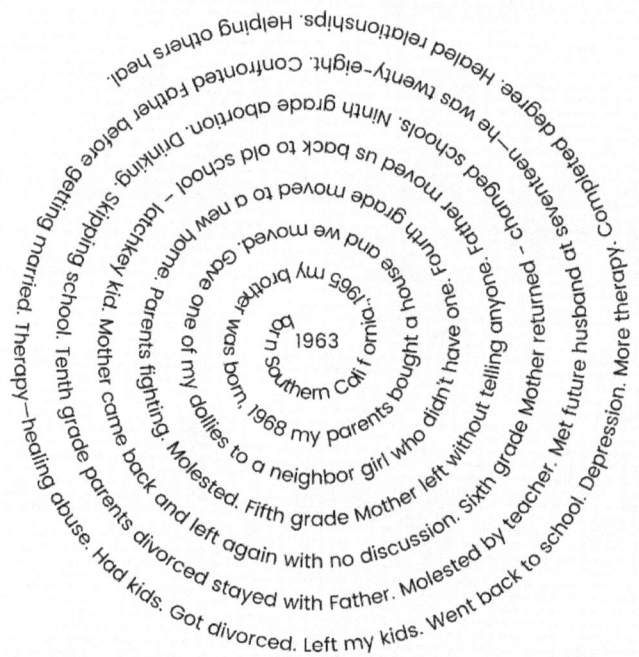

The spiral you create will show the trajectory of your life, but it's not over. Your life will continue to evolve whether you're aware or unaware of what you're doing. When you consciously engage in your healing process, you'll access the power to grow in the direction of your highest vision of yourself and your life.

Part One
Basic Understandings to Guide Transformation

Life isn't about finding yourself.
Life is about creating yourself.
~Lolly Daskal

Childhood sexual abuse can negatively impact your life far into adulthood, but the pain doesn't have to be a life sentence. Starting the transformation process can lead to many breakdowns because the psychological structures that hold the painful dynamics in place must break *down* before you can have a break*through*.

The saying "destruction before creation" might feel scary in the beginning because it *is* scary. The dismantling of old ways and old beliefs becomes easier as you remember the truth of who you really are and start reinventing your life from the inside out.

Knowing what you *do* want is just as important as knowing what you don't want. When I first become aware of changes I want to make, remembering "destruction before creation" helps me let go of what isn't working and identify what I can do to align with the future I want.

Tearing down existing walls in my home was a cathartic experience that helped me see all the invisible walls I built to protect myself from ever being hurt again.

> I own a home built in 1921. Homes built in the early part of the century had tiny kitchens. I love entertaining, but there was barely enough room for me to move around. I dreamed of having a spacious kitchen with tons of natural light and enough room for at least a small dinner party.
>
> Except for it being small, there wasn't anything wrong with my kitchen. There was a stove, refrigerator, and sink. I could get by. I told myself that I should be grateful for having a kitchen because many people don't have one. I thought a lot about what I wanted without taking any action to change anything. Instead, I felt resentful and stuck. Instead of feeling happy that I had a kitchen, I victimized myself with how cramped I felt.
>
> I had a choice. Being grateful, doing my best, and thinking positively wouldn't change my kitchen one bit. Thinking positively didn't give me the future I wanted and complaining just left me feeling powerless.
>
> Only tearing down the walls would make a difference. Removing the walls in my kitchen made a huge mess, but now there is light and room for me and my friends.

Destruction before creation is the same for reclaiming your life after childhood sexual abuse. It's messy. Tearing down the walls that I thought would protect me was difficult, but now there is light in my heart and I'm enjoying a level of freedom I never thought was possible.

If you want freedom from the past, then the walls must come down. What confines you today isn't the abuse, it's what you're telling yourself about the abuse. Getting free from the harmful experience of the past is what happens when you start questioning what you believe to be true. You can create anything when you let go of old habitual ways of thinking and make room for something new.

Throughout this book, I move back and forth between my personal and professional experiences. I share parts of my healing process so you can clearly see that I've gone through something similar to what you've experienced. I'm with you on our respective healing journeys.

I share the technical side of healing because you'll be more able to participate in your own transformation when you understand what keeps the pain and shame in place. The key concepts in this book will help you access personal power to free yourself from the residue of abuse. As you learn what keeps your pain alive, you'll shift from experiencing life through the lens of the abused child into the perspective of an adult survivor who has the capacity to learn how to thrive after abuse.

In the upcoming sections, I will be going over the following key concepts that will help you to skillfully engage in your own transformation:

- Traditional therapy and coaching
- Human development
- Clinical depression
- Getting help
- Trauma and the nervous system
- Four stages of transformation
- Experience biases
- A bucket with holes
- Identifying abuse
- Trapped in abuse
- Identity
- Inner Critic
- Be your own best friend

Traditional Therapy and Coaching

*Asking for help is never a sign of weakness.
It's one of the bravest things you can do.
And it can save your life.
~Lily Collins*

I have great respect for traditional therapy and have worked with excellent therapists at critical times in my life. I felt cared for by the therapists who helped me learn how to be kind and compassionate with myself as I uncovered the pain of my childhood experiences. I've also worked with exceptional coaches who lovingly and firmly guided me along my path.

There are many overlaps between coaches and psychotherapists, and both facilitate changes in the people they work with. However, there are significant differences in the professions which are important to understand when choosing what help to ask for. Traditionally, psychotherapists work with the mentally based issues listed in the *Diagnostic and Statistical Manual of Mental Disorders* (DSM-V). Therapists are trained to work with dysfunction and personality-driven issues whereas coaches deal with more complex issues which are not mentally based. You should pursue the support of a therapist instead of a coach if you're clinically depressed, suicidal, have a mental disorder, or are unable to maintain a basic level of functioning in your daily life. Therapists bring a wide range of skills and experience to help you heal.

Psychotherapists and coaches tap into the same theoretical models and techniques. The field of coaching is becoming increasingly sophisticated and effective, and psychotherapists are starting to add coaching skills to their practice. When using insurance to work with a therapist, the insurance company typically decides how many sessions will be covered based on a medical diagnosis. Not all psychotherapists take insurance. Typically, you pay for coaching out of your own pocket, but some companies will reimburse you through their Employee Assistance Program.

I created the chart below while interning for my master's in social work. The chart illustrates some commonly held differences between coaching and psychotherapy (adapted from Auerbach, 2000 and Gilligan, 2005) to help you decide which help to get.

Coaching	Psychotherapy
No presence of mental disorder	Presence of mental disorder
Alliance designed jointly and seen as a partnership—more client style	Alliance designed by therapist—more doctor/patient style
Client is seen as fundamentally healthy	Patient is seen as having a dysfunction
Coach keeps things focused and moving, interruptions common to keep on task	Emphasis is less on keeping things moving or on task; Interruptions less common
Forward action oriented	Feeling or insight oriented
Less strict boundaries with occasional self-disclosure and not uncommon to be involved in social situations	More strict boundaries with little self-disclosure, and very uncommon to be involved in social situations with client
Goals are clear; Sessions are goal-directed and future oriented	Goals are amorphous; Sessions are not goal-directed
Tools: inquiry, accountability, goal setting, planning, in person, phone, or a video program	Tools: listening, reflecting, confronting, interpreting, face to face in a special time and place

I needed help to see where I was stuck. I needed help to see how I was keeping the hurt alive. I needed help to change my life. I started my healing journey believing someone else created the prison I was in; but with help, I learned that I have the keys to free myself, and you do too!

It takes determination and persistence to get free, and you don't have to do it alone. Needing help is universal, so don't judge yourself. In general, survivors of childhood sexual abuse have difficulty asking for help because the people they trusted are the ones that were the least trustworthy. You might have been avoiding asking for help, but now it's time to tear down the walls that get in your way, take a risk, and go for it. You're worth it!

Types of Therapies

I find non-traditional therapies, such as Hakomi—Mindful Somatic Psychology, art therapy, and sandplay therapy to be effective because they work with the subconscious and allow healing to happen in an organic intuitive way.

Hakomi—Mindful Somatic Psychology

Hakomi is an experiential, mindfulness-based, and body-centered approach used to guide you to access your body's own wisdom. Created by Ron Kurtz, the Hakomi methodology helps to uncover unconscious relational patterns and beliefs so that you can create healthy and safe relationships. Healing and integration from past trauma can happen quickly. Current neuroscience research shows Hakomi's use of mindfulness, loving presence, empathic attunement, and limbic resonance to be an effective therapy.

Art Therapy

Art therapy, introduced by Adrian Hill in 1942, uses the creative process to communicate what might be too difficult to put into words. The resulting artwork is then used to help make empowered meaning out of your experience. Art therapy blends psychotherapeutic techniques with the creative process to tap into your unconscious wisdom and bring about healing and integration from past trauma.

Sandplay Therapy

The World Technique, or Sandplay, is a therapeutic intervention developed by Dr. Margaret Lowenfeld to help people who have suffered trauma. Sandplay is based in Jungian psychology and uses the subconscious mind to create scenes using a small sandbox and toy figures which are then explored with the therapist using talk therapy.

The above methodologies access the psyche's intelligence and natural impulse to heal itself.

If you choose to work with a therapist, I encourage you to seek out a trauma-informed therapist, and if a specific type of therapy is not helping you, then explore the options until you find one that does.

Here are just a few more therapies to consider:

Eye Movement Desensitization and Reprocessing Therapy (EMDR)

EMDR, developed by Dr. Francine Shapiro in 1987, doesn't require you to explain the traumatic event. You focus on an image related to the trauma and use eye movements and tapping to unstick your brain so your brain can complete the healing process.

Cognitive Processing Therapy (CPT)

Dr. Patricia Resick developed CPT in the late 1980s to help women survivors of sexual assault. CPT focuses on reevaluating how you think after a trauma. The focus is on how you view yourself, others, and the world around you. CPT helps you assess the impact of the trauma on your thinking. This therapy is very helpful if you feel a lot of shame about what happened to you.

Internal Family Systems (IFS)

Dr. Richard Schwartz developed Internal Family Systems in the early 1980s. The goal of IFS is to help people identify and accept the different parts of themselves so they can heal the wounded parts. You learn how to make friends with all the different parts of your Self so you can heal your wounded parts and come into a balanced whole.

Ecopsychology

Theodore Roszak coined the term Ecopsychology, also called nature therapy. Ecopsychology uses nature and outdoor activities to improve your mental health and well-being. Nature therapy can help reduce anxiety, anger, and depression.

Human Development: Models and Identity Formation

Many abused children cling to the hope that growing up will bring escape and freedom.

But the personality formed in the environment of coercive control is not well adapted to adult life. The survivor is left with fundamental problems in basic trust, autonomy, and initiative. She approaches the task of early adulthood—establishing independence and intimacy—burdened by major impairments in self-care, in cognition and in memory, in identity, and in the capacity to form stable relationships.

She is still a prisoner of her childhood; attempting to create a new life, she reencounters the trauma.
~Judith Lewis Herman, Trauma and Recovery: The Aftermath of Violence—From Domestic Abuse to Political Terror[1]

In the most general sense, we can understand identity to mean how a person sees and relates to themself. Your identity is formed in early life and is influenced by various people and circumstances. Childhood sexual abuse distorts your self-image, and you grow into adulthood forgetting who you really are.

To understand how sexual abuse impacts human development it can be helpful to be aware of the various theories and models of how people develop and change throughout life.

---

[1] Basic Books, 1992

Here are a few I find helpful:

1. Vygotsky's Sociocultural Theory says our interactions with other people play a significant role in our psychological development. The messages we get from early caregivers and how they relate to us impact our view of ourselves and the world.

Since our identity is formed in childhood, we're limited in what we create depending on the stories we tell ourselves and the meanings we make about who we are and the world around us.

2. Bowlby's Attachment Theory is based on survival instincts and is largely a function of the care a child receives in their early years. Children with a secure attachment feel secure in exploring the world around them and generally grow into confident adults who experience a sense of security and love. Children without a secure attachment have more difficulty as adults.

Research shows there's a significant impact in the ability to create healthy adult attachment in children who experienced trauma. If you're having difficulty in your adult relationships, an attachment wound could be the cause. Fortunately, it's possible to develop a more secure attachment style and experience healthy and satisfying relationships.

3. Maslow's Hierarchy of Needs says we progress through five stages of needs in the order of the most primal needs being met first.

Your physiological, or biological, needs must be met before your need for safety can be met. I've noticed myself moving through these stages in succession, with some stages taking longer than others, and some stages overlapping in the progression. As a survivor of childhood sexual abuse, you may not know how to create safety for yourself; however, you *can* learn.

4. Erikson's Psychosocial Development Theory says that a person develops their personality in eight organized stages from infancy to adulthood. The failure to complete a stage impedes further development.

Erikson's theory spans a lifetime. A child's development can be interrupted when there is a crisis such as childhood sexual abuse. Fortunately, each stage can be resolved as you heal.

Clinical Depression

*You say you're "depressed"—all I see is resilience.
You are allowed to feel messed up and inside out.
It doesn't mean you're defective—
it just means you're human.
~David Mitchell,* Cloud Atlas

Given the ways abuse gets internalized, it's understandable that people who have experienced childhood sexual abuse may also experience mild to severe depression at least once in their lifetime.

It's important to get help if scary feelings become invasive and get in the way of daily living. I'm proof life gets better after doing the work and getting free from the past so I could see more clearly the reality of what I had been through. It took effort to see I wasn't flawed because of the abuse and to understand more clearly it was the lens through which I was viewing my life that was flawed.

Let's do an assessment to help you become aware if you're experiencing depression. If you are clinically depressed, then you can get help like I did.

Gap Work: Online Depression Self-Assessment

This Gap Work requires you to take an online self-assessment for depression. Search *depression test* to access an online assessment tool.

The most common symptoms of clinical depression include changes in your daily life experience such as:

- A change in sleeping habits—either insomnia or sleeping too much.
- A change in eating habits—significant weight loss or weight gain.
- A change in interest or pleasure in normal activities.

Signs of clinical depression also include:

- Unexplained physical problems or emotional outbursts.

- Trouble thinking, concentrating, and making decisions.
- Frequent thoughts of death or suicide or suicide attempts.

Take the assessment.

Does the assessment show that you're clinically depressed? If so, or if you have any of the signs listed above, make an appointment with a therapist so you can get the support you need. If the results show you need help right now, please put this book down and call the National Suicide and Crisis Lifeline at 988. You can also text HOME to 741741.

Getting Help

...the most successful and accomplished people are those who can show courage and admit they can't do it alone.
~Brittany Burgunder

Early in my process, I felt intense shame asking for help. I felt isolated and alone. I believed I should know what to do without any guidance, so initially I didn't ask for help. Honestly, I didn't know how to describe what happened to me. I simply didn't have the words for it. I hope by reading this book you will learn how to say what you need to say without shame. Getting help, even if you don't know what to say, will make your journey a lot easier. Once I learned that giving myself support was a gift that helped me heal faster, I was all in.

There were times when a friend or spiritual teacher was the best choice and other times a therapist or a coach was the best choice. Knowing the support each provides can help you decide which help might be best for you at each stage of your journey.

Friends who give unconditional love and support are at the top of my list. I always want a good friend in my corner who listens without judgment. As I've grown and changed over the years, some friends have fallen away and new, friends have shown up to meet me where I am. If you don't give up, and you continue to seek out people who treat you well, you'll eventually find the right friends to be with you along the way.

I've had a spiritual teacher for many years now. She's my beloved guide along the path of awakening. I trust her and I'm nourished by her presence and encouraged by her loving support. Most importantly, she's helping me get freer from the impact of my early wounding. If you find comfort and support in your religious or spiritual path, then you'll have a lovely foundation for your healing journey. If, on the other hand, you've been harmed by a religious or spiritual teacher, then give yourself permission to seek out other support for now.

Trauma and the Nervous System: The Window of Tolerance[2]

You cannot predict the outcome of human development. All you can do is, like a farmer, create the conditions under which it will flourish.
~Sir Ken Robinson

Understanding how your nervous system works can positively impact your ability to stay present during periods of dysregulation. The window of tolerance, developed by Dr. Daniel Siegel, describes how arousal affects the capacity to function in daily life.

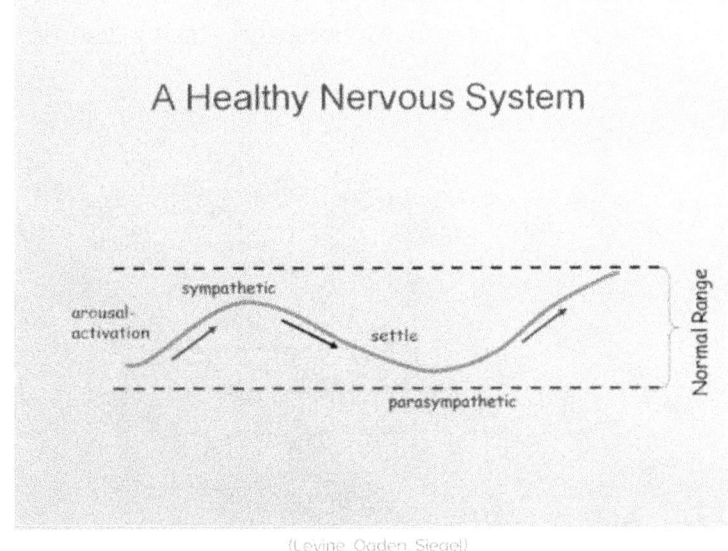

(Levine, Ogden, Siegel)

The previous image shows a healthy nervous system where you can think and feel at the same time. Inside the two dotted lines represents an optimal window of

---

[2] https://www.gov.je/SiteCollectionDocuments/Education/ID The Window of Tolerance 20 06 16.pdf

tolerance. Being able to think and feel at the same time is what makes it possible to respond appropriately to everyday life challenges.

When your nervous system is healthy, you'll have a large window of tolerance, and you won't be distressed by the ups and downs of life. You might get agitated, upset, or disappointed in difficult circumstances, but you'll easily come back to a settled nervous system. Inside a healthy nervous system, it's easier to make decisions and respond to whatever is happening in life without getting out of balance.

Traumatic events temporarily impact the nervous system. When a person experiences trauma, they move outside of the window of tolerance and lose the ability to consciously respond to what is happening in current time. Even if you need counseling after a traumatic event, a wide window of tolerance allows you to find balance and return to balance relatively easily and quickly after a trauma.

People who have been sexually traumatized as children tend to have a diminished window of tolerance. Some survivors experience post-traumatic stress disorder (PTSD). PTSD is a diagnosis showing a severely compromised window of tolerance. People with an extremely narrow window of tolerance tend to have an over-emphasized need to control what happens in their environment to feel safe even when nothing truly threatening is happening. Strategies to stay inside the window of tolerance include obsessive-compulsive behaviors, eating disorders, and anxiety around other people's behaviors.

Let's look at a dysregulated nervous system:

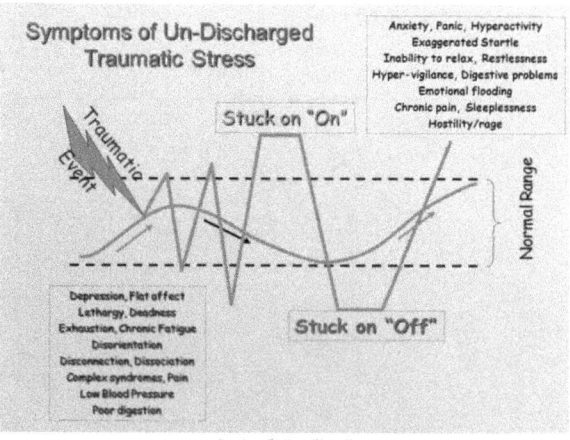

Most people move outside of their window of tolerance when there's a traumatic event. The wider the window of tolerance a person has, the more of life's ups and downs a person can tolerate. When a person exceeds their capacity, they'll get thrown out of their window of tolerance. The line above the window of tolerance shows the hyperarousal state where there's a more volatile reaction to the event.

Hyperarousal includes actions like yelling and bullying, road rage, and crimes of passion. The line below the window of tolerance shows hypo-arousal states where there's more of a collapsed reaction to the event. Hypo-arousal includes a "deer in the headlights" freezing or pulling the covers over your head to disappear.

In both the hyperarousal and hypo-arousal states, a traumatic event causes you to lose your capacity to think through your actions. The difference between a healthy and unhealthy nervous system is that someone with a healthy nervous system can manage their daily life without getting thrown out of the window of tolerance and will come back into their window of tolerance after a trauma, whereas someone with an unhealthy nervous system, or narrow window of tolerance, may not come back fully into their window of tolerance at all.

When I experience a real or imagined threat of abandonment, my tendency is to go into hypo-arousal and shut down. With the awareness I have today, I rarely get outside of my window of tolerance. But in the past, I would freeze if someone was upset with me. I felt utter terror which made no sense for what was happening at the time. Whenever I was faced with a potential relationship loss, I was transported back in time—not to the experience of abuse, but to the sensation in my body that felt the same as the terror I felt when the abuse happened.

When I'm outside of my window of tolerance, I can't form a sentence. My throat constricts, and I lose access to my voice. The pain is intense. It's difficult to breathe, and I literally gasp for air. When I've been in this type of trauma response, no matter how hard I tried to say something, no sound came out. Every time this happened, I felt like I was going to die. My mind would go blank, and I acted like a cornered animal. I wanted to fight, but I couldn't move.

I've learned how to widen my window of tolerance, and today I experience the freedom of responding to life in ways that are appropriate for what's happening in each moment.

A wide window of tolerance is connected to feeling at ease in your body whereas a narrow window of tolerance is connected to dis-ease in your body. Let's take a few minutes to assess your window of tolerance. Be assured that if you have a compromised—or narrow—window of tolerance, you can learn how to widen it, but you have to know where it is first.

Gap Work: Assessing Your Window of Tolerance

*The one constant law of the world
is that it would heal.
~Brenna Yovanoff*

Get out your journal.

Make a short list of difficult experiences you've had over the last week.

Take about twenty minutes to think about how you react in difficult situations. Knowing whether you get angry and lash out or get quiet will help you determine whether you tend to go into hyperarousal or hypo-arousal.

For each event, notice if your reaction is habitual and automatic or if you respond to each situation from awareness. Ask yourself:

- What do I do when I'm upset?
- What do I do when I'm scared?
- What do I do when someone hurts me?

Do you remember when you first felt broken? Or first lost connection with yourself?

> The first time I remember feeling broken was while the abuse was happening. It felt like I had been shattered. I went into hypo-arousal and shut down. It was like a part of me left my body.

Ask yourself:

- When was the first time my window of tolerance was impacted? What happened?

The more you know when you're in or out of your window of tolerance, the more power you'll have to widen your window of tolerance.

Ask yourself:

- What happens when I'm *inside* my window of tolerance?
- What happens when I'm *outside* my window of tolerance?

Having a wide window of tolerance allows for clear thinking and staying present with everything that happens in your life. Learning how to widen the window of tolerance begins with bringing awareness to your reactions and how you respond in normal daily circumstances. As you engage with the exercises in this book, you'll naturally widen your window of tolerance. Notice how being able to respond rather than react to daily circumstances increases as you engage in the exercises. Track your progress in your journal and stick with it.

Four Stages of Transformation

If you change the way you look at things,
the things you look at change.
~Wayne Dyer

There's a world that's available to you where you're free from the impact of childhood sexual abuse, where you can more easily create healthy and safe relationships, and where you're authentically happy. To claim this future, you have to step outside of your comfort zone and see what happened to you from a new perspective. You'll need to engage in new ways of thinking and feeling about yourself and what happened to you and take actions that align with a future you've only dreamed of.

I guarantee you can create that future if you fully engage in your growth. When you understand how change happens, then you can consciously pursue your freedom. In 1969, Martin M. Broadwell developed a teaching model to describe the process of acquiring a new skill. I apply his learning model to the process of returning to wholeness after childhood sexual abuse. The four stages of transformation are Unconscious Incompetence, Conscious Incompetence, Conscious Competence, and Unconscious Competence.

Let's look at each of these stages in the context of transformation.

Stage 1: Unconscious Incompetence

Unconscious Incompetence includes everything you're unaware of. At this stage, a person feels victimized by life and whatever happened to them in the past. They feel powerless and doubt they have any control over what happens to them in the future.

People in Unconscious Incompetence believe they aren't responsible for anything that is happening in their lives. They think they can't move forward until external circumstances or other people change. During this stage there's an unconscious drive to keep life as status quo through complaining and ruminating about what isn't working.

You can tell someone is in Unconscious Incompetence if they're unaware of being deeply embedded in the dynamics of codependence where there's an imbalance in their relationships. An imbalance can be recognized when one person gives much more than their partner even though both people have the same capacities. Imbalances bring feelings of resentment and anger and cover up a deep sense of unworthiness. People in Unconscious Incompetence are often unaware of their own needs. If a person is unaware of their needs, they get expressed in unspoken expectations making it impossible for other people to meet their needs.

The hallmark of Unconscious Incompetence is blame. Blame shows up as a lack of awareness and a feeling of victimization.

Answer these questions to see if you're in Unconscious Incompetence:

- Do I blame what happened in the past for the conditions of my life today?
- Do I keep having the same experiences in my relationships and believe it's always the other person's fault?
- Do I often feel like others should know how I feel? Or how to behave even though I haven't shared directly with them?

While it's important to hold people accountable for the harm they caused, at this stage survivors view life through a victimized lens blaming other people for the current quality of their life and the negative things that repetitively happen.

You can't return to wholeness and authenticity if you stay in Unconscious Incompetence. Evolving out of Unconscious Incompetence takes courage and a willingness to stop blaming others for the external conditions of your current life. Evolving beyond the disempowering stage of Unconscious Incompetence is only possible when you're willing to let go of victimization.

I've been in Unconscious Incompetence. I was absolutely convinced if my husband would only be different, then I would be okay. I blamed his drinking for why our relationship wasn't happy. I blamed him for working too much and not investing in our relationship (the way I thought he should). I blamed him for not wanting to grow and change with me (the way I wanted him to). I blamed him for not having emotions and for not being attuned to my feelings and needs (the way I thought he should). I complained to my friends and family and felt justified and supported in believing my husband was the problem. I felt relieved to know our problems weren't my fault.

When I was in Unconscious Incompetence, I chose someone who I believe needed to change for me to be happy. I couldn't see I was responsible for being unhappy by choosing to stay in a relationship that wasn't giving me what I needed. It wasn't *his* fault I stayed in the relationship waiting for him to change and believing everything would be okay once he did. At this stage, I felt completely powerless.

For many years (in Unconscious Incompetence) I also believed the abuse was the reason I didn't have a happy relationship. Only with awareness could I see that the reason I didn't have a happy relationship was because I hadn't learned the skills to create something healthy. Once you're aware that you're responsible for your life, you can move from Unconscious Incompetence into Conscious Incompetence.

Stage 2: Conscious Incompetence

The hallmark of Conscious Incompetence is an increased awareness and a feeling of shame. Conscious Incompetence happens when you become aware that the choices you make are what keeps you stuck. Power is found in recognizing how you participate in engaging in unhealthy patterns or staying in an environment where it's impossible to thrive.

It's in Conscious Incompetence that you become aware that the quality of your life and relationships *are* your responsibility, but you don't know how to go about creating what you want. Emotional pain comes with the realization you've participated in creating your current dissatisfying circumstances. Staying unconscious is a way of avoiding emotional discomfort; however, there's no access to personal power until you're willing to wake up from a victimized trance and take responsibility for creating the life you want.

Inside of Conscious Incompetence it's common to stop blaming others and slip into shame. Shame kept me stuck and feeling alone for years and ultimately led to clinical depression. Moving from blame to shame is a step in the right direction because it indicates a movement toward your potential to create a thriving life; however, shame will only keep you stuck in pain, so don't stop with shame.

Like I did, you may experience a considerable amount of regret when entering the stage of Conscious Incompetence. But keep going with confidence that you're changing your life for the better. Immerse yourself in awareness and take advantage of the organic movement toward possibility. Learn all you can about yourself and the world around you so you can get free. Becoming responsible for your future takes more effort than blaming someone else. While it's hard to take responsibility, the results will be well worth the endeavor.

I felt shame admitting to myself that I created my current reality, but nothing will change until you become aware of what you're doing.

Here are some of the ways I was responsible for the quality of my relationship:
- I knew my husband was a heavy drinker before we got married, but I chose to marry him anyway.
- I chose someone who prioritized his drinking over his relationship with me. I also prioritized his drinking over my own needs, making it easy for him to drink. I drank with him.
- I chose to stay with my husband even after he made it clear he wasn't interested in growing and changing with me.
- I stayed in the relationship with him even when I knew he didn't have any interest in caring for me the way I needed to be cared for.

Here's how you can tell if you're in Conscious Incompetence:
- You shift the blame to yourself, telling yourself, "It's all MY fault."
- You know you created the problem but don't know how to fix it.
- You might feel embarrassed for staying in situations too long.
- Recognizing your responsibility for a pattern of behavior, you might be immobilized by shame.

At the Conscious Incompetence stage of transformation, it's important to continue to raise your awareness. Learn all you can by educating yourself. There are many books, classes, and workshops that can help you get free. It would be wise to hire a coach or therapist to guide you away from shame and toward increased responsibility.

Stage 3: Conscious Competence

When you're in the Conscious Competence stage of transformation, you've learned the ways childhood sexual abuse impacts your life today, and you've acquired the skills needed to create a healthy and safe life. It takes effort at the stage of Conscious Competence where you must consciously and consistently use everything you've learned and make different choices. Forgetting, even for a moment, can return you to old patterns.

It's during Conscious Competence where there are many new experiences to celebrate. For example:
- An increase in confidence around feeling whole and complete as you are.
- You take more risks to show up as your authentic self.
- Codependence is disappearing and you start setting healthy boundaries with others.
- You're paying attention to the causes and effects of your choices.
- You let go of relationships and situations that are not good for you.

Everything started to change when I decided to take responsibility for my own life, but it was scary in the beginning to take an action that I hadn't ever taken before.

> I was seven months pregnant with my daughter and was sick for most of my pregnancy. We were at a party at my in-laws' and, as usual, my husband was drinking. I suffered for as long as I could before letting him know how bad I was feeling and that I needed to go home and rest. It was a two-hour drive home, and it was already late in the evening. My husband informed me that we would leave after he finished the beer he was drinking, but three beers later, he still wasn't finished. He embarrassed me in front of everyone, telling me that if I wanted to go home I should do so without him. So, I did. I took care of myself even though there would be consequences that I was terrified of, like losing the relationship. My husband found his own way home the next day and didn't talk to me for two weeks.
>
> Before that pivotal experience of prioritizing my own well-being, it was easy to put myself last. Making the choice to drive home that night to take care of myself was one of the early choices I now recognize as the seeds for the happy life I'm living today in which I choose to be in relationships only with people who also prioritize my well-being.

My fears of abandonment and rejection kept me in Conscious Incompetence. I didn't know how to take a stand for myself and in the beginning, and every time I did, it felt like I was putting my life at risk. There's no other way; you must step outside of your known way of being and take actions that are aligned with the future you're creating.

During Conscious Competence I worked hard to not blame my husband or shame myself for the choices we each made. With awareness I eventually discovered that it would be best to leave my marriage. It took effort to not blame him or shame myself and remember that wanting something different didn't mean we didn't love each other. It just meant we weren't a good fit for each other. While it was scary leaving the relationship, we're both happier today. And I'm happy to share that today he now treats me with the utmost respect and care.

Here's how you can tell if you're in Conscious Competence:

- With effort, I can stay present with myself and others.
- With effort, I am neither blaming others nor shaming myself.
- With effort, I'm bringing compassion to myself and others.
- With effort, I'm taking responsibility for what is mine and letting go of what isn't.

Another hallmark of Conscious Competence is the need for the right effort in applying your newfound awareness and everything you've learned. It takes a great deal of life-force energy to keep showing up in new ways. Opening communication, staying present (instead of dissociating) when there is conflict, setting boundaries, saying no, and facing fears of abandonment all require effort in Conscious Competence. If you stick with it, you'll discover what I did: The effort in being authentic leads to deep intimacy and satisfying (and safe) relationships with yourself and others.

As you put in the effort to keep making new choices, the evidence of the life you're creating will fuel your journey to the final stage of transformation.

Stage 4: Unconscious Competence

The hallmark of Unconscious Competence is that you no longer need to think about using the tools you've learned. You'll know you're in Unconscious Competence when you've integrated everything you've learned and are now living free from the unconscious impact of childhood sexual abuse; you'll have a new healthy habitual way of being which is authentic to you and where you're effortlessly creating healthy relationships; when there are upsets in relationships, you address them directly without assigning a negative meaning. You'll know you're in Unconscious Competence when there's a sense of flow and ease in navigating difficult situations. When you're in Unconscious Competence, it's easy to stay present with yourself and others without feeling drained.

Answer these questions to determine if you're in Unconscious Competence:

- Am I creating healthy relationships without having to think about it?
- Do I easily set boundaries with myself and others?
- Do I let myself contribute and be contributed to equally?
- Do I find compassion and kindness have replaced blame and shame?
- Can I easily hold multiple perspectives without judgment?
- Do I find I no longer take things personally?
- Is it easy for me to let others have their experience without the need to defend or deflect?

While childhood sexual abuse will always be part of your experience in this lifetime, you're no longer unconsciously recreating the felt experience of the abuse. You may still fall back into old patterns during intense periods of disappointment, trauma, or loss; however, you'll have the capacity to bring yourself back to Unconscious Competence quickly.

Gap Work: Assessing Your Stage of Transformation

> *You can learn new things at any time in your life if you're willing to be a beginner. If you actually learn to like being a beginner, the whole world opens up to you.*
> ~Barbara Shur

Get out your journal.

I always wanted to be further along the journey than I was, but avoiding being where I was only got in the way of getting the help I needed to get to the next stage of my transformation. Knowing the stage of transformation that you're in can help you see where you're stuck and what area to work on.

Take about twenty minutes to assess what stage of transformation you're in. Include any insights you gained from contemplating each of the four stages of transformation.

Growth and an Evolving Truth

> *Nothing is predestined. The obstacles of your past can become the gateways that lead to new beginnings.*
> ~Ralph Blum

When I first start working with a client, one of the first things they tell me is they want to start being true to themselves. My clients are aware that they're self-abandoning but don't know how to stop. The key to authenticity is to replace hiding with vulnerability.

Vulnerability is not an emotional meltdown. You become vulnerable through self-reflection and being honest with yourself and others. As you reflect on your life, you will find many ways that you create your own limitations. For example, if you believe someone in your life doesn't make you a priority, but you don't let them know how you want them to make you a priority then you'll continue to create a world where they don't make you a priority.

Everything changes when you get real with yourself, but to stop unconscious patterns of thinking, feeling, and behaving from getting in the way of creating something new, it's vital to make the unconscious conscious.

Initially, shame made me hide myself. I hid the parts of myself I believed nobody would accept or love—the parts that aren't perfect, the part that has needs, and the part that's insecure about my value. Fear of abandonment continued into my adult relationships. I hid my power because I believed that people would leave if I was too powerful for them. I hid myself to protect myself from being abandoned, but hiding only distanced me from the support, love, and connection I desperately wanted.

The survival strategies I developed to avoid rejection all centered around self-abandonment. I was good at knowing what other people needed and gave it to them before they asked. I became an expert helper at the expense of my own needs. I lost connection with myself and didn't know how to change what wasn't working in my life. Shame was like a cocoon I lived in but couldn't let anyone know how broken I felt.

Questions like the ones below breed shame and are generally not helpful:

- Why does this keep happening?
- Why can't I change this?

If you can see when you're blaming or shaming yourself, then you'll have more power to stop it. See if you can reflect on your life as it is today without falling into blame or shame. Instead, objectively look at the choices you're making without making yourself wrong.

As you grow and evolve, so will your understanding of what's true. Now that you're doing the hard work to uncover what's true today, it's time to gather everything you discovered so far into one place.

Gap Work: What's True Now?

It's never too late to become who you want to be. I hope you live a life that you're proud of, and if you find that you're not, I hope you have the strength to start over."
~F. Scott Fitzgerald

Get out your journal and plan a few days to contemplate what you've discovered about what's true right now. You can't make changes until you're aware of what needs changing, so use everything you've revealed in the previous exercises to be as objective as possible and be encouraged by what you see. Go back through the exercises in this section and make a list of what you discovered. Don't get discouraged if you have a long list, it just means you have the awareness needed to make lasting changes in your life.

You've navigated many experiences in your life. Write them down. Below are some examples of what might be here now. You can circle the ones you experience and add to them. Include your difficulties and challenges.

- I had a difficult childhood experience that left me feeling broken and unworthy.
- A part of me feels afraid to stand up for myself.
- I have difficult emotions which I don't know how to deal with.
- It's hard to stay connected to my body in times of stress.
- I blame myself for what happened and what is not working in my life.
- I believe I should be able to change things easily.
- I continue to have unhealthy intimate relationships.
- I have the need to control everything to feel safe.
- I have the habit of giving to others at my own expense.
- I feel inadequate in making the changes I need to make.

Include how you've grown or how you've developed yourself. Include the smallest to the largest successes, and things you think were like *Oh, that was nothing*.

- I have developed strength and a capacity to make things happen.
- I'm confident in who I am and what I have to offer in many situations.
- I contribute to friends and family in authentic ways.
- I'm learning how to be kind and gentle with myself when I make mistakes.
- I give myself permission to learn and grow without expecting more from myself than I can reasonably do.

- I'm connected to my feelings and needs most of the time.
- I take good care of my body.

Include the qualities you currently have access to.

- I've developed many wonderful qualities, including courage, strength, perseverance, kindness.
- I have the capacity to learn and grow.
- Even though I'm scared, there's a part of me that knows I'm okay.

Include what you've been able to change or create.

- I have a healthy relationship with my sexuality.
- I have ended codependence in my relationships.
- I have very difficult conversations around sexual abuse.
- I have created a friendly respectful relationship with my ex-partner.
- I have a successful career.

Include where you need to grow.

- I know I need to make the changes, and I'm ready to get help.
- I need help connecting with the truth of who I am more consistently.
- I need to learn how to set healthy boundaries.
- It's difficult for me to forgive, and I don't even know if I want to.
- I'm too hard on myself and need to learn how to hold myself with compassion.
- I feel drawn to develop qualities including forgiveness, gratitude, and discernment.
- I'm ready to heal the trauma from my childhood.

Include anything else that's here now whether it feels positive or negative.

Now answer these few questions:

1. What help do you need? Coaching or therapy?
2. If the depression assessment shows you're clinically depressed, are you willing to get help from a therapist?
3. What models of healing are you drawn to?
4. Do you need help widening your window of tolerance?
5. What stage of transformation are you in? (Unconscious Incompetence, Conscious Incompetence, Conscious Competence, Unconscious Competence).
6. What did you discover completing your evolutionary spiral timeline?
7. What most needs to change?

Experience Biases

*People will generally accept facts as truth only if
the facts agree with what they already believe.*
~Andy Rooney

Experience bias is the tendency to believe something based on previous experience. The tendency to interpret new experiences as evidence of the belief you made up when you got hurt deepens into false beliefs. False beliefs develop into your core identity in adulthood.

Core identities are the "I am" of who you are. Core identities are deeply connected to self-worth and self-esteem that begins developing in childhood.

Here are some commonly held ideas around false beliefs, identity, and behavior:

- Your identity is who you believe yourself to be.
- What you believe about yourself drives your behavior.

You have the power to shift your core identity in two ways:

1. When you change what you believe about yourself, your behavior will change.
2. When you change your behavior, what you believe about yourself will change.

Core identities become rigid and are difficult to change until you challenge the meaning you made of past experiences. Changing what you believe about yourself first is the more difficult path to shifting your core identity. I recommend changing your behavior and the habitual ways you show up in life first. When you change your behaviors, then you'll get feedback from your environment that tells you if you're on the right track or not. As your experience changes, your beliefs will organically follow.

Let's take a step and identify what behaviors need to change so you can start having new experiences.

Gap Work: Identifying New Behaviors

If you always do what you've always done, you'll always get what you've always gotten.
~Henry Ford

Get out your journal and make a list of new behaviors you know you need to change or the ways you wish you could easily show up in your life. Here are some ideas:

Old behavior: I treat my body like I don't care about it. I don't drink any water; I don't exercise with any regularity; I ignore my body when I know I should see the doctor.

New behavior: I treat my body like I care about it. I make sure to drink at least ½ my body weight (pounds to ounces) in water, I exercise at least three times per week, and I see the doctor for regular checkups to make sure I'm in optimal health.

Old behavior: I take care of everyone except myself. I'm tuned into other people and meet their needs without having to be asked. I drop what I'm doing to help someone. I rarely, if ever, let people know what I need or ask for help. If I say no, I feel guilty.

New behavior: I prioritize myself and my own needs. I take the time to tune into myself and make sure that my needs are met. I wait for people to ask for help and only help when it's not at my own expense. I ask for help when I need it. I have learned how to say no without feeling guilty.

Old behavior: I stay in relationships with people when I know they are not good for me. I let people treat me badly. I withhold my truth thinking things will change without doing anything. I let my partner make all the decisions. I don't even know what I want.

New behavior: I leave relationships when I know they're not good for me. I set boundaries and don't let anyone treat me badly. I share my truth and take action to change what isn't working. I make decisions in collaboration with others. I take the time to know what I want and let others know what's important to me.

Any new behaviors you engage in will eventually leave you feeling like you matter, but changing your behaviors feels scary and risky. In the beginning the new behaviors will feel awkward, but they're just unfamiliar and you need to be patient with yourself.

It's in The Gap where you'll practice new ways of showing up. Acting in ways that are different from what you're used to may be one of the most difficult things to do, but it's the only way to guarantee a new outcome. Behavior must change if you want a different outcome and as you experience a different result, it will become easier to make the changes that were previously difficult for you.

A Bucket with Holes

> *Thought changes structure... I saw people rewire their brains with their thoughts, to cure previously incurable... trauma.*
> ~Norman Doidge

How you see the world is different when there's abuse. Prior to abuse, the way a person thinks about themselves is like having a bucket of water. If there are no holes in your bucket, then it takes no effort to keep your bucket full. When there are no holes in your bucket, it's easy for you, or someone else, to add water to your bucket.

If you don't have any holes in your bucket, then in your life, you'll:

- Think highly (and realistically) about yourself and what you're capable of.
- Not make disempowered meaning of what other people do or don't do.
- Create healthy interdependent relationships instead of unhealthy co-dependent relationships.

After abuse there are holes in your bucket and you won't be able to keep your bucket full no matter how hard you try. You'll wear yourself out trying to keep your bucket full. Others who try to contribute to your bucket will become exhausted trying to help keep your bucket full.

If you have holes in your bucket, then in your life you'll:

- Think harshly of yourself. You'll criticize yourself and compare yourself to others.
- Make disempowered meaning of what other people do or don't do.
- Create unhealthy codependent relationships instead of healthy interdependent relationships.

Unintegrated childhood wounds are like having a hole in your bucket. The main hole in your bucket represents the meanings made early in life when you were harmed and weren't given the love, care, or consideration when you needed it the most.

The interpretations children make are simplistic because children don't have the capacity to think with much complexity. Instead, children internalize abuse and make someone else's behavior mean there must be something wrong with them which caused the abuse. Then children grow up without correcting the interpretations they made.

Instead of correctly interpreting the sexual abuse as someone else's lack of responsibility, capacity, care, or simply someone's bad behavior which caused the harmful impact, children make what someone did to them mean something like:

- I'm unloved.
- I'm alone.
- I'm unsafe.
- I'm invisible.
- I'm bad.
- I'm not good enough.

The Cost of Having a Hole in Your Bucket

> *The responsibility for success is on you; so is the responsibility for creating meaning out of life's biggest disappointments.*
> *~Thomas Koulopoulos*

While it took an enormous effort, repairing the hole in my bucket was one of the best things I've ever done. Today, I feel deeply loved and cared for and now I have a true sense of my own value. I'm finally free from the pain and shame of childhood sexual abuse.

False beliefs and subjective meanings of past abuse are reinforced through unconscious thoughts and actions in current time. When you understand how the hole-in-the-bucket thinking shows up in daily life, you can begin to make the repairs to your bucket. First, you need to clearly see how the false belief hole-in-the-bucket thinking shows up in your life.

Here are some of the costs of the hole-in-the-bucket thinking in my life:

- The cost was my happiness. Instead, I experienced clinical depression.
- The cost was not having healthy relationships. Instead, I had unbalanced, codependent relationships.

- The cost was not feeling safe in the world. Instead, I let people take advantage of me putting myself in dangerous situations.
- The cost was to my peace of mind. Instead, I took the abuse personally and made it mean that I didn't matter.

Gap Work: What Is Your "Hole in the Bucket" Meaning?

The wholeness and freedom we seek is our true nature, who we really are.
~Jack Kornfield

Get out your journal. Set aside fifteen minutes to identify the meaning you made when you were first hurt. Your hole-in-the-bucket meaning will likely be quite easy to identify because it's the most recurrent negative belief you have about yourself. If you have more than one hole-in-the-bucket meaning, then write them all down. If you don't know what they are, just give it your best guess for now.

I made it mean *I don't matter*. What did you make it mean?

Write down the meaning you made about what happened.

Once the interpretation is made, you have a hole in your bucket and no matter how much someone tries to prove they love you, it will never be enough. Someone can show you love in many ways, but the moment they do something that doesn't feel like love to you, you'll discount all the previous ways they loved you and interpret their actions to mean they don't love you now and probably never did.

Their love will drain out of the bottom of your bucket leaving you feeling the same way you felt when you were first harmed.

Holes in buckets have severe consequences. My hole in the bucket was a belief I didn't matter, and it cost me years of happiness. The hole in the bucket cost me being able to create a fulfilling intimate relationship. It prevented me from being real with the people closest to me. I compensated for how poorly I felt about myself and treated everyone else like they mattered more than I did. My hole in the bucket got in the way of my peace of mind and sense of belonging.

Write the cost of having a hole in your bucket.

Identifying Abuse

*There will come a time when you believe everything
is finished; that will be the beginning.*
~Louis L'Amour

Working for the Center for Domestic Violence, I saw an enormous number of women (and some men) seek help to get away from abuse. I used the Wheel of Power and Control and the Wheel of Equality (below), developed by the International Abuse Prevention Project, to help people experiencing domestic violence discern between abusive and healthy behaviors.

I use these same charts to teach survivors of childhood sexual abuse what constitutes abusive behaviors. Many people who have survived childhood sexual abuse aren't aware (Unconscious Incompetence) that what they are experiencing as an adult is abuse. Becoming aware that what is happening to you is abusive (Conscious Incompetence) opens the door to make changes to stop the abuse (Conscious Competence) and go on to create healthy relationships (Unconscious Competence).

Below are two charts to raise awareness of the difference between healthy and unhealthy relating.

Ellen Pence, Michael Paymar, and Coral McDonald created the Wheel of Power and Control after working extensively with battered women. The Wheel of Power and Control is used nationwide in centers for domestic violence to help women see themselves as victims of abuse. Take a close look at this wheel and notice if there are any experiences you've had.

DOMESTIC ABUSE INTERVENTION PROGRAMS
202 East Superior Street
Duluth, Minnesota 55802
218-722-2781
www.theduluthmodel.org

You're not alone if you didn't know the behaviors in this chart are abusive. If you're currently experiencing any of the violence in this chart, consider talking to a therapist.

To people who were abused as children, abuse can feel so familiar it seems normal. People learn what's normal, not what's healthy and right, from how caregivers treat them. Survivors of abuse often live with a skewed sense of what it means to be loved. Abuse is often the result when you don't know the difference between healthy and unhealthy relating.

Also developed by the International Abuse Prevention Project, the Wheel of Equality represents healthy relational behaviors.

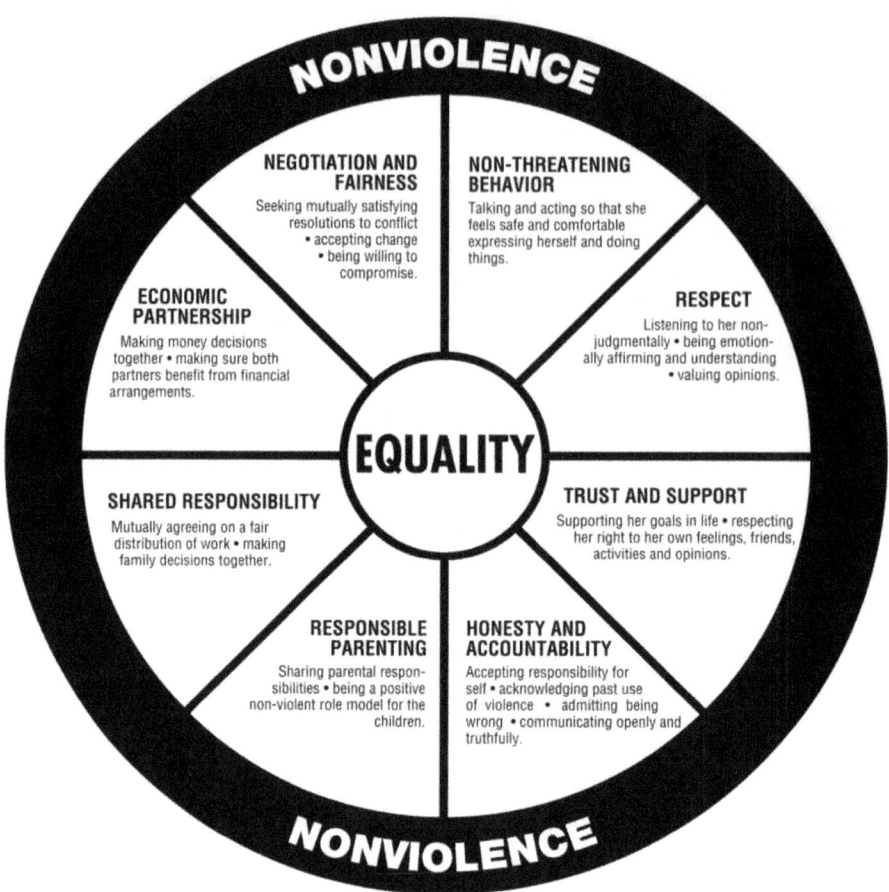

Gap Work: What Behaviors Do You Experience?

Some people think that the truth can be hidden with a little cover-up and decoration. But as time goes by, what is true is revealed, and what is fake fades away.
~Ismail Haniyeh, Palestinian political leader

Get out your journal.

The charts above have the power to move you from not knowing you're being abused (Unconscious Incompetence) to identifying abuse that happened or is happening in your life, and not knowing how to change it (Conscious Incompetence). Acknowledging the patterns in yourself may be difficult, but doing so will help move you forward on your healing journey.

Start by reviewing the two charts.

- Highlight the behaviors you experience from each of the above charts.
- Differentiate between past and present experiences.
- Take twenty minutes to journal about what you noticed.

Now make a list of the ways you were hurt.

Were you sexually abused? Sexual abuse includes rape, molestation, and incest.

Were you emotionally abused? Emotional abuse can include many things, like not being believed if you told someone about the abuse. Emotional abuse can be at the hands of a parent, caregiver, clergy, or other relatives or people (like a sibling or friend) who have authority or power over you.

Here are some examples of emotional abuse:

- Being threatened if you tell someone about the abuse.
- Being told the abuse is your fault.
- Being given adult responsibilities as a child.
- Being put in the middle of parental disputes.
- Being humiliated, minimized, or habitually criticized.
- Being made to do degrading things.
- Being the subject of caregiver's jokes.

Were you neglected or abandoned by a parent or caregiver?

Neglect includes not being cared for physically. Were you not given proper nutrition? Did you come home to an empty house after school? Were you not guided around proper hygiene?

Abandonment includes a parent or caregiver leaving and not maintaining a relationship. Human beings are wired for connection. Having a consistent caregiver provides us with a felt sense of security and belonging in the world. If you were abandoned, you may experience inconsolable emotional pain in your body. Were you abandoned? Were you left to take care of yourself younger than you should have been left?

Trapped in Abuse

Life is ten percent what you experience and ninety percent how you respond to it.
~Dorothy M. Neddermeyer

What I believed about myself changed the day I was molested. I was left feeling shocked, confused, and deeply ashamed. One moment I was at the center of a life where I knew how deeply I mattered to everyone. The next moment, my confidence was crushed. I unconsciously interpreted being molested to mean I didn't matter anymore.

Children make being sexually abused personal by creating a meaning for why the abuse happened. The meaning feels true, but it's not. The meaning a survivor makes about the abuse continues until they stop taking it personally. With awareness, anyone can more accurately interpret what happened and when they do, their healing process will gain momentum.

Here are some examples:

- Instead of accurately interpreting that someone I trusted hurt me, I made it mean I wasn't loved.
- Instead of accurately interpreting that someone took advantage of my vulnerability, I made it mean I was unworthy.
- Instead of accurately interpreting that my father did something wrong by using his power over me, I made it mean I was bad and there was something wrong with me where I would cause him to do what he did.
- Instead of making it mean that I was violated, I made it mean I didn't matter.

Gap Work: What Do You Make the Abuse Mean?

Getting over a painful experience is much like crossing monkey bars. You have to let go at some point in order to move forward.
~C. S. Lewis

Write here what you made the abuse mean about you:

I made what happened to me mean _____.

Being able to accurately interpret what happened leads to freedom from the secondary harm of believing something which isn't true.

It's not true that I am unloved.

It's not true that I'm unworthy.

It's not true that I'm powerless.

It's not true that I'm bad.

It's not true that I don't matter.

What you just wrote isn't true either. It's not.

Use the meaning you wrote above to complete this sentence:

It's not true that _____.

Limiting false beliefs *feel* true. Getting to the source of false beliefs requires time for self-reflection. Even with an advanced logical understanding, it can be difficult to get past the bodily felt sense which makes you believe whatever you made up about yourself at the time of abuse.

Identity

People are like stained-glass windows. They sparkle and shine when the sun is out, but when the darkness sets in, their true beauty is revealed only if there is light from within.
~Elisabeth Kubler-Ross

Your identity is based in part on the roles you play in your life, which are extensive. For example:

- Mother, daughter, sister, aunt, niece.
- Father, son, uncle, brother, nephew.
- Teacher, student, boss, employee.
- Friend, partner, spouse, provider.
- Entrepreneur, mentor, activist.

Another aspect of identity includes the meanings you make about yourself. One way to identify your "meaning" identity is to listen to what you tell yourself in the privacy of your own mind. Here are some common "meaning" identities that I've either told myself at certain times or have heard from clients:

- I'm stupid.
- I'm a failure.
- I'm worthless.
- I'm bad.
- I'm unlovable.

These "meaning" identities or false beliefs go to the core of who you know yourself to be and what you believe you can or cannot have in life. False beliefs harm you and get in the way of living your full potential. To get free of false beliefs, you need to recognize them as lies you've told yourself and start telling yourself what's true about who you are. When you change what you believe about yourself, then you change your experience at the level of your identity.

As a child, believing I didn't matter was internally devastating and excruciatingly painful as I recreated this belief throughout much of my life. My misguided thinking where I believed I didn't matter impacted the choices I made for decades to follow. I believed I had to prove I was important and found myself striving for perfection, yet success never left me feeling like I mattered. Instead, I felt compelled to get as much validation from the external world as I possibly could, and it was never enough.

I unconsciously used my sexuality to feel like I was important, and I collapsed when my sexuality wasn't enough to create both a healthy sexual relationship and a meaningful non-sexually intimate connection with a partner. As hard as any of my partners tried, nobody could love me enough to patch the gaping wound created in my childhood. It was like having a hole in my bucket I couldn't keep full no matter how hard I tried.

Initially it may be hard to believe, but unless the abuse is happening in this moment, it only exists as a memory. The residue of abuse lives in the body and can get triggered during everyday life circumstances. What happens in current time gets filtered through an inner child's interpretation, making it difficult to assess your adult reasoning about what's happening right now. Gaining freedom from what you believe about the abuse requires being able to differentiate between the abuse that happened a long time ago and what you tell yourself about the abuse in current time.

What happened is over. What you tell yourself about what happened is your story. You can let go of the story, you can forgive, and you can move on; however, abuse will still have an impact on your life. With increased awareness, you can update the story and make new choices that are aligned with the life you want to create. The result will be a new empowered story to tell that lessens the impact of past abuse.

Stopping the belief that I *don't* matter and treating myself like I *do* matter made it possible to create the life I have today where I am confident in knowing how deeply I matter. Aligning myself with a new story that "I matter" led to making choices which ease the impact of past abuse on my life.

Here are a few of the new choices I'm making:

- I let potential partners know my deal breakers early so we don't waste each other's time.
- I only have sex after knowing my potential partner and I want the same things.

- I share what matters to me and ask for my needs to be met. If my partner isn't available to meet my needs then, after a discussion, I leave the relationship.

Making the above new choices makes it possible for me to decide whether I want to continue getting to know a potential partner before becoming too emotionally invested in the relationship. All the choices I make contribute to the story of my life and what I believe to be true.

The tendency to relate to life through a story about the past is a natural part of being human, which keeps one inside of victimization. Fortunately, with awareness, what you believe about the abuse can be overcome, and you can create something new.

I learned how to separate what happened to me from the meaning I was giving to what happened and I learned to create a life which transcends the impact of childhood sexual abuse. My life today is now filled with safety, reliability, and authenticity.

Shame and pain related to sexual abuse can feel like a steel cage around the throat keeping the person who experienced childhood sexual abuse silent and in denial. Becoming conscious of the "false belief" story running in the background is essential in gaining freedom from the past.

You may always be impacted by the past, but you don't have to be defined or limited by it. Stay present to the fact the initial harm isn't happening now, and you'll move toward freedom more easily. Bringing awareness to the beliefs you created because of the abuse makes it possible to get free of the gravitational pull of early childhood beliefs.

Hold these two ideas at the same time to start creating a new operating system:
- You are not responsible for what happened to you as a child.
- You are 100 percent responsible for what you do with what happened to you.

Holding these two ideas simultaneously leads to being compassionate for the ways you were victimized while at the same time owning your power to create a happy, healthy future for yourself no matter what difficulties come your way. Everyone deserves compassion and kindness around past abuse. However, habitually commiserating with others to get sympathy for what you experienced will, unfortunately, deepen feelings of victimization.

> I complained to a friend about an injustice I experienced but wasn't doing anything to change it. Honestly, it felt good to receive her sympathy and outrage at how I had been mistreated. She obliged me for almost two years before she stopped me. I'm forever grateful to her for telling me she was done hearing me cry about what happened to me. While her candidness surprised me at first, it shocked me into taking responsibility for what I was giving my attention to.
>
> She was right. Once I stopped giving energy to the story I was telling, I moved on to conversations which were more worthy of my life-force energy and that could bring about the change I wanted, and I created a new story for my life.

Do you want to be known as the victim or victor? How you experience your past is found in the story you tell. Here's an exercise to raise awareness of the story you're telling so you can consciously choose which story you want to be known for.

Gap Work: Telling Stories

We don't own events or their reasons. We own what we do with them.
~Thomas Koulopoulos

No matter how you tell it, your story has creative power. Most people tell their story in a way that solidifies their past into what feels like an absolute truth of their false belief. The following exercise helps create distance from your story by relating to what happened to you from pure energy instead of recreating the painful victimized experience that telling your story in words creates.

Get out your journal. Set a timer for five minutes. Write as much of your abuse story with as many details as possible before the timer rings. This is not the time to take responsibility. Let your victimized voice speak. Write about how the abuse is the reason for what isn't working in your life today. When the timer rings, stop writing.

Now tell your story out loud three times in succession.

Story #1—Set the timer for two minutes. Tell your story as if you were telling a friend who hadn't heard it before. Make sure to tell it in a way which makes your friend feel sorry for you.

Story #2—Reset the timer for two minutes. Tell the same story as if it were the funniest thing that ever happened to you. Take the full two minutes.

Story #3—Reset the timer for two more minutes. Tell the story as if you were a dog. Bark your story. Let the energetic feelings come through in animal language feeling your story as pure energy.

Get out your journal again and write down what you notice.

- What am I aware of as I tell my story in these different ways?
- Is there anything shifting around my story?
- What, if any, different feelings am I experiencing?

Let's tell your story one more time. Set the timer for two minutes. Tell your story as if what happened to you is the best thing that could have ever happened. Tell the story from your wise self that is strong and confident in who you are and why you're here. Stand strong with both feet flat on the ground, your head held high, and shoulders back and away from your neck. Breathe into your belly while you speak.

Go back to your journal and write down what you notice.

Inner Critic: A Bullying Storyteller

I woke up today and thought, "Enough is enough with bullying myself." The war is within you and that's also where it's won.
~Keala Settle

Everyone has an Inner Critic, the bullying storyteller. For some the Inner Critic is a relentless voice that traps you in your head where a habitual conversation dominates your life. Many people believe the Inner Critic is trying to keep them safe or help them do better, which I do not believe is true. The Inner Critic is mean. It's an abusive tyrant who does not deserve your respect or kindness. The Inner Critic is a voice who tells you what you're doing wrong, how you're unloved, that you're not measuring up, or that you're a pathetic failure. The Inner Critic compares and separates you from yourself, your own humanity, and other people who also experienced sexual abuse when they were a child.

You can identify the shaming tactics of the Inner Critic when you hear yourself asking these questions:

- Why is this happening?
- Why am I feeling this way?
- Why can't I...?
- Why does this always happen?

Asking *why?* keeps you attached to the Inner Critic and stuck in emotional pain. It's extremely hard for survivors of childhood sexual abuse to answer *why* questions accurately because the question *why* is asked from the lens of the false belief created at the time of the abuse, it leads to unhealthy destructive storylines, and it's self-abusive.

Listening to the Inner Critic takes you out of your body and into your head where a habitual inner conversation can dominate your life. If you let it, the Inner Critic will destroy you like it almost destroyed me.

I was doing my best to hide what I was going through from everyone in my life. I spent most of my days staring at a computer screen listening to the harsh voice inside my head.

Family members expressed concern with my weight loss—I lost thirty pounds in a few short months and weighed barely a hundred pounds. I dismissed my family's concern and kept right on starving myself. I wasn't sleeping. Prescription sleep aids were ineffective, and I started hallucinating.

I didn't know I was clinically depressed. When the nonstop judgmental Inner Critic began encouraging me to take my own life, I started calling suicide prevention during my morning walks. The volunteers answering the phone helped save my life.

I started working with a therapist and with her guidance, I realized I had to stop the Inner Critic before it killed me. Going up against the Inner Critic felt like a superhuman feat—a battle of wills. My therapist took me on a guided journey to face off with my Inner Critic.

I closed my eyes and imagined the Inner Critic standing in front of me. While it was berating me, I took out an imaginary samurai sword and cut its head off. To my horror, my Inner Critic immediately grew another head and kept right on disparaging me.

My assignment was to have a zero-tolerance policy for the Inner Critic and to cut its head off every time it opened its mouth. Over the next three weeks I exhausted myself cutting its head off at least five hundred times a day. Keeping this boundary took all the energy I had as I fought for my life, and thankfully, I won.

While I still have an Inner Critic, its head is the size of a tennis ball, it speaks in a high-pitched squeaky voice, which is impossible to take seriously. Where I was once afraid of my Inner Critic, today my Inner Critic is afraid of me. It lives on the other side of a mountain range making its shenanigans literally irrelevant in my life.

In the absence of the Inner Critic, I eat and sleep well. I have compassion for myself and no longer compare myself to others. I'm happy and content being free of that abusive voice.

Gap Work: Stopping the Inner Critic

Boundaries define us. They define what is me and what is not me. A boundary shows me where I end and someone else begins, leading me to a sense of ownership. Knowing what I am to own and take responsibility for gives me freedom.
~ Henry Cloud

When I worked for the Center for Domestic Violence, I accompanied women to court hearings where judges issued restraining orders. In every single case, the judge explained that a piece of paper had no power to keep anyone safe. The judge advised the people I worked with that for the protection order to be effective, they would need to enforce it by calling the police if it was violated.

If you don't stop the Inner Critic, nobody else will. You must treat the Inner Critic like the abusive bully it is. Take your power back by following these four steps:

1. Commit to a zero-tolerance boundary around listening to the Inner Critic.
2. Decide on how you'll stop the Inner Critic. You can use my samurai sword, or you can choose any method you're willing to follow through with.
3. Make a decision to not listen to the voice of the Inner Critic ever again. Every time you hear the Inner Critic, use your chosen method to stop its voice.
    a. When you hear the voice, try saying this: "That's the voice of my Inner Critic. I'm not listening to it any longer."
4. Be consistent and don't give up.

In contrast to the abusive Inner Critic, you can call forward your Inner Best Friend as a guide on your journey back to wholeness. You can tell the difference between the Inner Critic and your Inner Best Friend because your Inner Best Friend will never judge you. They'll hold you accountable with a kind firmness. Your Inner Best Friend is kind and compassionate and will uplift you and deepen your sense of connection and interdependence.

The Inner Best Friend is a healthy, caring grownup you can trust. Your Inner Best Friend will get stronger as you turn away from the Inner Critic and turn toward her.

Be Your Own Best Friend

*Your relationship with yourself sets the tone for
every other relationship you'll ever have.*
~Robert Holden

Most survivors of abuse treat themselves like an enemy instead of a friend. As a survivor of childhood sexual abuse, you probably have many missing experiences such as:

- Knowing you matter to the people closest to you.
- Being loved in healthy ways.
- Feeling supported and protected.
- Being treated with respect and consideration.
- Having caregivers go out of their way to ensure your safety.
- Being cared for by thoughtful, loving adults.

While you can't go back in time to have these experiences, you can learn how to give them to yourself in present time.

The adult part of you can learn how to create safety for yourself by treating yourself like you would treat your best friend. The positive effects of treating yourself like you really care will ripple throughout all your relationships. It's in your best interest to learn how to treat yourself well. Start today with making a sacred commitment to treat yourself like your own best friend.

Gap Work: Best Friend Commitment Meditation

*When you are your own best friend, ... you realize
that the only approval and validation you need is
your own.*
~Mandy Hale

This exercise invites you to make a deep commitment to yourself; this lifetime commitment will open the doors to your heart in ways that will consistently deepen your relationship with yourself so you can care for yourself in the best way possible.

Set aside twenty minutes where you can sit quietly with yourself. Have your journal and a pen close by as you may want to take notes during this meditation.

> Close your eyes and bring attention to your breath. Feel the rise and fall of your chest. With each breath, feel the air enter in through your nose and hit the back of your throat. Draw your breath all the way down into your belly and fill your belly with air.
>
> Notice how gently your breath leaves and enters your body. Stay with it for several breaths and place your hand on your heart.
>
> Imagine you are in a beautiful safe place in nature and, with your eyes closed, take a look around.
>
> Notice there is a meditation cushion which has been made especially for you. Maybe it's a stump of a tree or a big rock. Maybe it's a cloud or a large chair. Whatever shows up, it's a comfortable place made just for you to rest and be still.
>
> Claim this as your space. Make your way over to your seat and settle in.
>
> Coming back to your breath, call forward the part of you who knows how to be a best friend. This is the part of you who loves you deeply and unconditionally. This is the part of you who knows all the difficulties and joys you've experienced. This part of you knows your insecurities and loves you anyway. They understand the deeper meaning of everything that happened in the past and chose to come into this life to help evolve your soul.
>
> This is the part of you who knows all the mistakes you've made, the shame you've felt, and extends only compassion toward you. This part is completely committed to you and knows who you really are. This is the part of you who wants you to be happy and successful and prosperous. This part wants your highest good and supports you fully.
>
> Take a few breaths and connect with this part of you, noticing what this part looks like and how they carry themselves.
>
> Imagine they're walking toward you and notice the energy this part of you carries.

Invite them to sit across from you and acknowledge this is the part of you who sees you as their best friend.

Looking into the eyes of this part of you, take a breath together and ask this part of you to give you their name, other than your own, and a quality they represent. Perhaps it's Compassionate Casey or Loving Linda.

Now ask this part of you to show you the cost of not committing to yourself, of not treating yourself like a best friend.

Does it cost your happiness? Your self-esteem? Your ability to connect with your highest self? Does it cost you your joy?

Notice, without any judgment, what it costs you.

Take another breath and ask this part of you, "What action can I take today which will support me in treating myself like my own best friend?"

Listen and take a few notes.

Ask this sacred part of yourself, "What do I need to know for me to fully commit to myself as my own best friend? Listen for the answer.

Now ask, "Is there anything else I need to know right now?" Write down whatever you hear without censoring yourself.

Now, look into the eyes of this part of you and repeat these words to yourself:

"I make this commitment to you. To take you as my best friend forever and to treat you with kindness and respect. I commit to loving you and supporting you in your time of need. I'll play with you often and rest when you need a break. I'll laugh with you when you're being too serious. You don't have to be perfect with me. I love you no matter what. I'll be real with you and with others. I'll be brave in showing up fully as myself. And I will make this commitment each day of my life."

Let this part of you respond and feel the commitment you're making and how it's always been available, even if you didn't know it.

Now, invite this part of you to say whatever you've longed to hear about how loved you are, how you belong to this part, and how worthy you are.

Take a few more slow deep breaths, and when you're ready, open your eyes.

Take a few minutes to write in your journal what you discovered. Be sure to write down your commitment to be your own best friend.

NOTE: You can find audio for this guided meditation in the resources section on my website. Follow this QR code to visit LeilaReyes.com/FreedomfromShame:

Part Two
The Impulse to Heal

In order to be who you are, you must be willing to let go of who you think you are.
~Michael Singer, The Untethered Soul

Most people are thrilled when they get engaged to be married. They're excited at the promise of an exciting new adventure. They're thinking of a life of love. They're anticipating a future happy family. Not me; I was terrified.

When my fiancé and I decided to get married, a black cloud appeared blocking the joy that was supposed to finally be mine. Instead of being excited about becoming a wife and mother, I worried something bad was going to happen. I felt an anxiety I hadn't felt since the sexual abuse which happened to me years earlier.

While I wanted to be married and start my new life, I didn't care about a wedding dress or beautiful venue or where I would spend my honeymoon. I was scared. Underneath all the buzzing excitement, I was preoccupied with a fear no one should have to be concerned about.

I was thinking about how to protect my future children and prevent them from being hurt the way I had been hurt.

And for the first time, I spoke about the abuse. Not to a friend, not to my fiancé, not to a therapist but sitting across from the person who hurt me—my own father. And my healing began.

Survivors of childhood sexual abuse grow into adulthood with well-established coping mechanisms. Children sometimes suppress their memories to keep themselves safe. Children sometimes disconnect from their bodies, or dissociate, to protect themselves from the pain of what happened to them. These unconscious coping mechanisms are brilliant in childhood, but unfortunately don't work to heal the past or create a healthy adult life.

The desire to make the abuse go away is normal. Some adult survivors of childhood sexual abuse distance themselves from their family to attempt to make the abuse go away. The desire to get far from the abuse is normal and natural, but leaving the family you grew up in won't stop the dynamics from happening again in your new relationships. Stopping the cycle of abuse takes more than distancing yourself from the people who hurt you, it takes conscious effort.

The impulse to heal and return to wholeness is what motivates people to enter The Gap and heal themselves. As an adult, the impulse to heal happens when you become aware that you can no longer live with abusive patterns in your life. Since you can't make the abuse go away, the only option is to stop letting the past define you. You must stop letting what hurt you get in the way of creating the life you want. You must stop aligning with the wounded part of you and start aligning with a future that reflects your fully healed whole self. To heal, you need to take risks and acknowledge what happened—first to yourself, then to others.

I was terrified when I first confronted my father. It was easy to ignore my past until I started planning for a family. As soon as having children became a possibility, I knew at the core of my being I had to risk everything for my unborn children and be willing to walk away from my family if it meant protecting my future children.

You can heal beyond the abuse by accessing powerful qualities, including:

- Courage
- Acceptance
- Presence
- Humor
- Motivation

Evolving beyond abuse includes stepping outside of blame and shame. Healing beyond abuse will give you power over the past and the clarity to see the choices you're making today which keep you stuck in old familiar patterns.

People who have been abused as children often have a difficult time discerning what is and isn't their responsibility. Learning the difference of what is and isn't your responsibility will help you make choices that are right for you. For example, you're never responsible for someone's choice to abuse you, but you're always responsible for the life you create as an adult after abuse.

Your Support System

Realize that you are not alone, that we are in this together, and most importantly that there is hope.
~Deepika Padukone

Survivors of abuse are chronically under-supported and tend to lean toward doing it alone. Being under-supported is a symptom of the belief about your own unworthiness to have support. It can feel like an external reason that others aren't there for you, but it's more likely that you've unconsciously created your own lack of support.

A support system is a resource that helps you make changes in your life. A support system includes people like friends and family members, a therapist, and/or a coach. A support system includes books that guide you along the way and programs like codependents anonymous.

Here are some clues regarding your beliefs around not giving yourself the support you need:

- Do you feel ashamed of needing help, so you never ask?
- Do you reject help when it's offered?
- Do you give up instead of seeking out the help you need?
- Do you use the excuse you can't do something because you need help, but never find the help you need?
- Do you have unrealistic expectations you *should* be able to do it all yourself?

I felt incredible shame around needing help and could answer "yes" to the above questions until I was well into my healing. In the beginning I had to step out of my isolated comfort zone and force myself to get help. Once I started seeking help, I realized how supported and loved I was. Most important, I learned how to let go of what wasn't working and find support that was truly helpful.

Gap Work: Your Support System.

> *Be strong, be fearless, be beautiful. And believe that anything is possible when you have the right people there to support you.*
> *~ Misty Copeland*

It's time to assess the support you already have, the support you need, and change the support that is no longer helpful. Keep adding to your list as you discover additional support you need.

Let's start with your beliefs around support. Understanding your relationship to needing support will make it easier to create a support system which works for you.

What are your BELIEFS around the need for support?

- How does "needing support" make you feel?
- Do you expect to get support, or do you believe it won't be there for you?
- What support do you secretly long for but have a hard time asking for?

What support do you currently have?

- Who are the people supporting your life? Be sure to include family, friends, and professional support.
- What structural support do you have? Be sure to include how your basic needs for food and shelter are met. Include any financial support through work or gifts.
- What support do you wish you had? Include financial, emotional, and professional support.

Everyone needs support, but it can be difficult to discern between support which empowers growth and support that's not helpful. Answering these questions can help identify destructive support which isn't really support after all:

- Who discourages you from growing?
- Who refuses to respect your boundaries?
- Who minimizes your feelings and needs?
- Who gives you advice which leaves you feeling incapable or insecure?

We are often harder on ourselves than anyone else is. Notice if you're a member of your own discouragement committee and make a commitment to become your own number one supporter.

In what ways do you *not support* yourself? Include comparing yourself to others, calling yourself names, and putting yourself last on your priority list.

There are many feelings which come with not giving yourself the right support, including:

- Feeling like a failure.
- Feeling overwhelmed.
- A lack of confidence.

Over time, cultivating the voice of compassion changes the way you speak with yourself. It takes time to get good at being hard on yourself, so it will take time to get good at being kind and supportive toward yourself.

Call in Your Support System

> *Asking for help isn't a sign of weakness, it's a sign of strength. It shows you have the courage to admit when you don't know something, and to learn something new.*
> *~Barack Obama*

There are many kinds of support you may need on your healing journey. Let's look at what support you need to start giving yourself.

Let's start with identifying any structural support you might need. Structures are like containers which help us to move forward. Some structures that can be helpful are:

- Using this book to guide you through a healing and growth process.
- 12-step programs.
- Regular routines like meditation or exercise.

Make a list below of the structures you feel would support you in making consistent progress.

The structures that would be good for me are:

Now let's look at the professional support you might need. Professional support can provide clarity around what needs to change and how to authentically make those changes. A coach can help precision the changes as you continue to integrate what you're learning.

Make a list below of professional support, like a coach or a therapist, who you feel would be a good support for you.

The kinds of professional support which would be good for me are:

Now let's look at the people you need to support you. Changing your life becomes easier with feedback from people around you who are committed to your growth. A nonjudgmental friend can reflect the learning which is happening and give you opportunities to try new techniques as you integrate new skills and capacities into daily living.

Make a list below of people you feel would be a good support for you. Include supportive friends and family. Only include people who respect your boundaries.

People who could be a good support for me are:

Now it's time to get the support you need.
- Commit to at least one structure that will support you as you work through all the exercises in this book.
- Reach out to the people you listed and ask if they're available to support you. Be sure to clearly let them know the kind of support you're asking for.
- Contact the professional support you need. Schedule initial meetings to find a coach and/or therapist who you resonate with.

You can schedule an introductory session with me at LeilaReyes.com.

Now take about ten minutes to write in your journal about giving yourself the support you need. Include how you feel about taking this important step and what you imagine your future will be like when you have the support you need.

Identifying Your Growth Edge

*Change can be scary, but you know what's scarier?
Allowing fear to stop you from growing, evolving,
and progressing.*
~Mandy Hale

A growth edge is an area of your life you know needs to change. Growth edges are uncomfortable and require an accurate naming of what's holding your current experience in place. Growth edges are uncomfortable and often require outside help to navigate.

Knowing where you're stuck can help identify your growth edge. Knowing what isn't working and needs to change is one of the easiest ways to see where you're stuck. Let's take some time to bring awareness to the areas you most want to change.

Gap Work: Identify Your Growth Edge

*Nothing in the universe can stop you from letting
go and starting over.*
~Guy Finley

Get out your journal and answer these questions.

- What beliefs about myself hurt me the most?
- What parts of myself do I *not* want anyone to know about?
- What do I most want to change about my life?
- Where do I feel most stuck? And what do I think keeps me stuck?
- What patterns keep happening no matter how hard I try to stop them?
- What boundaries do people keep ignoring?

Take about five minutes and write about anything else that you don't like about your life as it is today.

Now that you've identified what isn't working for you, let's take some time to look at what you would most enjoy in your life.

- What do I most want to believe about myself?
- What do I most want to experience in my life?
- What do I long to experience in my closest relationships?
- What qualities do I admire in other people? And how do I want people to think about me?
- What boundaries do I most want people to respect?

Healing the trauma of childhood sexual abuse requires that you start doing things differently than you have in the past. Here are some uncomfortable growth edges:

- Putting the Inner Critic in its place.
- Staying in your body and not dissociating when you feel afraid.
- Creating true intimacy with yourself and others.
- Setting healthy boundaries.

Using what you discovered from the above exercise, make a list of the changes you would like to make in your life.

The changes I would like to make in my life are as follows:

1.
2.
3.

These are your growth edges. Write these changes in your journal.

Setting an Intention

The great secret of getting what you want from life is to know what you want and believe you can have it.
~Norman Vincent Peale

Creating unlimited possibilities for yourself and those you love starts with knowing what's important to you. If you know what you want, then you can create it. My initial motivation for healing was wanting my children to have a safe grandfather, so my future children were the catalyst to start my healing journey. The desire for a healthy and safe family free of sexual abuse inspired me to find the courage to enter The Gap and confront my internal fears, which unconsciously ran many aspects of my life, including my romantic relationships.

Your life can look any way you want it to if you're willing to name what you most desire and then do the work to align yourself with that future vision of your life. I generated safety within my family because I wasn't willing to settle for anything less, and today, I have a thriving vibrant life with healthy relationships.

If you're not ready, it's okay to put this book down for now and try again later. If you are ready, however, then let's dive in and set an intention by looking at what's not working first.

Gap Work: What's Not Working?

Don't live the same year seventy-five times and call it life.
~Robin Sharma

Knowing what's not working can be helpful when creating an intention. Take a few minutes to answer these questions so you can clearly see what needs to change.

- What do you never want to have happen again?
- What do you never want to feel again?
- For each relationship, answer the following questions:
    - What is missing in this relationship?
    - What happens in this relationship that you're fed up with?
    - In what ways does this relationship leave you feeling similar to when you were a kid?
    - What do you most long to feel or experience in your relationships? What gets in the way of having this experience?
    - What have you not been willing to admit about this relationship?
- Where are you over-giving?
- What do you no longer want to do for others?
- What are you saying yes to which you don't want to do?
- What do you need to start doing for yourself? Maybe exercising, eating healthy, taking long walks, going back to school.
- What needs are best for you to prioritize? What are you doing instead?
- Who are you giving your time and energy to in ways which deplete you?

Turn what's missing into what you want by writing out the opposite of what you just wrote.

For example, if you never want to feel alone again, then "I never want to feel alone again" becomes "I want to feel deeply connected with myself and others."

Now write the opposite of each item that is missing for you, so you can see more clearly what you want to experience.

What Do You Want?

Nothing is impossible. The word itself says, "I'm possible!"
~Audrey Hepburn

Let's look at the quality of your relationships starting with the foundational relationship which supports all other relationships—the relationship you're having with yourself.

What do you want in relationship with yourself?

- Do you want to feel comfortable in your body and with your sexuality?

- In what ways do you want to trust yourself? What would your life look like if you did?
- Do you want to be confident in the choices you're making and the direction you're headed?
- How do you want to treat yourself?

What do you want to experience with an intimate partner?

- Do you want to be treated with respect and consideration?
- In what ways would you like to be cherished by a partner?
- Do you want to end co-dependence and be truly inter-dependent?
- Do you want a true partnership instead of feeling alone in your relationship?

What do you want to experience with friends and/or family members?

- What relationships would you like to have? Include family relationships, friendships, and any intimate partnerships.
- How do you want to feel when you're with family and friends?
- How do you want to be treated by family and friends?

What do you want to experience with your career?

- In what ways do you want to contribute to the world?
- How do you want to feel when you go to work?
- What have you always wanted to do with your life in regard to work?

Let's look at what you most want to experience in your life.

- What does your ideal life look like?
- How do you most want to feel about yourself?
- In what ways do you most want to contribute to the people in your life?
- What do you most want to receive from the people in your life?

Now it's time to set an intention that would be worth the work you're doing in this book.

What Is Your Intention?

> *We either live by intention or exist by default.*
> *~Kelly Armstrong*

Use everything you discovered from the last two sets of questions to clarify your intention. Answer these questions to identify what you most want for yourself and your life.

- What do I most want to experience in life?
- What do I most want to feel about myself?
- What do I most want to create for myself?

My first answers to the above questions were simple. What I most wanted to experience in this life was to be happy and to know I'm loved. What I most wanted to feel about myself is that I mattered. And what I most wanted to create for myself is connection with myself and others.

Your first intention might be what you want to get away from:

> My intention is to be free from the pain and shame I feel around sexual abuse.

See if you can turn what you want to get away from into what you want to go toward:

> My intention is to live a life of peace and high self-esteem.

Write your intention here:

> My intention is _____
>
> _____

My intention has grown over the years and yours will too. With a foundation which includes my early intentions of happiness and love, knowing I matter, and connection with myself and others, my intention has grown into the contributions I want to make. My intention embodies all my early intentions and over time yours will too.

Here is my intention today:

My intention is to cause humanity's awakening to their inherent wholeness where everyone honors the sacredness of life and is living their full authentic expression of love.

Don't feel bad if your intention is simple and all about your own healing. My first intention was simply to feel better. Keep the intention you wrote without any judgment, and it will grow with you. Like I have, you can update it as you learn more about yourself and what matters most to you.

Owning Your Intention

> *If you are working on something that you really
> care about, you don't have to be pushed.
> The vision pulls you.*
> ~Steve Jobs

Intentions are guiding lights. Staying connected with your intention on a regular basis will strengthen your commitment and bring awareness to what you most want. Return to your intention often and align your thoughts, feelings, and actions with the future you're creating.

Now that you have an intention, identify at least three ways you can make sure you connect with your intention every day. Here are some ideas:

- Write your intention on a sticky note and put it on your bathroom mirror.
- Create a screen saver for your phone or computer with your intention on it.
- Make a vision board.

Write down your commitment to connect with your intention.

Gap Work: Make a Vision Board

> *Our intention creates our reality.*
> ~Wayne Dyer

A vision board is a fun and personal way to make a visual representation of your intention. Once you finish your vision board, you can look at it every day to help you remember what you're committed to creating. Some people prefer to create an electronic vision board, but I like getting my hands on the images.

Here are some easy steps to create a vision board using physical magazines.

You can make your vision board very quickly or you can take a few weeks to complete it. Either way, set aside at least thirty minutes for your vision board session.

Step 1—Gather your materials.

- A poster board or piece of cardboard at least 24" x 36".
- Glue or tape.

- Scissors (optional).
- Pens.
- Music (optional).
- Gather images which represent what you want to create. Collect magazines with lots of images to cut or tear out. You can also print images from the computer.

Step 2—Connect with your intention.

Write your intention so you can easily see it while you're preparing for and creating your vision board.

Here are some ideas:

- Write your intention on large paper and stick it to the fridge with magnets.
- Update your computer with your intention as the screen saver.
- Write your intention at the top of the poster board you will use for your vision board.

Step 3—Put on some music (optional). Here are some ideas:

- "Brave" by Sara Bareilles
- "Let It Go" by Demi Lovato
- "Live Your Life" by T.I. featuring Rihanna

Step 4—Choose the images for your vision board.

Choose images which leave you with the *feeling* of how you imagine your life will be once your vision becomes your reality. While there are no rules for creating a vision board, I highly recommend you resist the temptation to include written words. Written words access the left, or analytical, side of your brain, whereas, images access the right part of your brain, or the creative-intuitive side—so focus on how the images make you *feel* instead of how they make you think.

Step 5—Arrange the images you chose on your board and apply them with glue or tape.

Step 6—Display your vision board where you will see it every day.

Aligning with Your Future

I believe we each have the opportunity to undergo thousands of little deaths and rebirths every day. Each time we do, we free up space to live more fully in tune with who we really are, and to go where we are being called to go.
~Laurie E. Smith, Spirit in Disguise: A Guide to Miraculous Living, Book 2

To create something different from what you've already experienced, you'll need to do something different from what you've already done. To bring your intention to life, you'll need to start aligning your actions with your intention—the future you want to create. Changing your habitual way of behaving feels awkward, unfamiliar, and scary in the beginning. Changing old ways of behaving can feel risky because you don't yet have enough evidence the new way will give you what you want.

Taking actions that you haven't before will become easier only after you've practiced new ways of showing up over time. The more you practice, the more evidence you'll collect. With consistency, you'll soon discover your capacity to align with your future has increased.

There's great benefit in taking risks. You may need to let people go who can't or won't get on board with the future you're creating. You may feel sad ending relationships which have been important to you, but it can also be exciting to finally have the tools to create the life and the kinds of relationships you long for. Either way, you'll need to take risks to make something new happen.

Gap Work: Taking Risks

Your life does not get better by chance.
It gets better by change.
~Jim Rohn

Get out your journal. Set aside fifteen minutes to write about the changes you need to make. After you write about the changes, answer the following questions:

- What am I afraid might happen if I make this change?
- What am I afraid of losing?
- What am I afraid of feeling?

And also:

- What am I hopeful might happen if I make this change?
- What am I excited about gaining?
- What am I looking forward to feeling?

Courage

You must do the thing you think you cannot do.
~Eleanor Roosevelt

Making a commitment to creating something new can bring up fear. I was terrified when I began my healing journey. It was difficult for me to know what I wanted, let alone take actions to create it. It was excruciating to speak what was true for me and stand up for what I wanted in the most basic ways. Fear shook my entire being, and at the time, I didn't understand what was happening to me.

Today, I know I was at my growth edge. I understand the beliefs I created as a child became the foundation for all my fears. Fears like:

- I'm afraid of being alone.
- I'm afraid of being hurt.
- I'm afraid of being rejected.

My fears led me to create a life where I believed other people mattered more than I did. The feeling in my body was an unspoken visceral terror where I believed it was TRUE that I didn't matter. I did everything possible to avoid feeling that pain and I unknowingly created strategies to prevent others from leaving me. Well, that didn't work.

My fears led me to abandon myself and my needs. I focused on everything outside of myself and found my value and safety in doing things for others so they wouldn't leave me. Everything changed once I became aware of what I was doing to avoid rejection. I have since learned how to relate to my fears in ways which don't interfere with the intentions I have for my life.

Gap Work: Naming Your Fear

Our deepest fear is not that we are inadequate. Our deepest fear is that we are powerful beyond measure. It is our light, not our darkness, that most frightens us. We ask ourselves, "Who am I to be brilliant, gorgeous, talented, fabulous?" Actually, who are you not to be? You are a child of God. Your playing small doesn't serve the world.
~Marianne Williamson

Most of what we do is unconscious. Human beings create strategies to avoid what they're afraid of, so to gain power over your fears, it's important to name what you're afraid of.

Make a short list here and in your journal of what you are most afraid of.

_____
_____
_____

Make a short list here and in your journal of what you do to avoid experiencing what you are most afraid of.

_____
_____
_____

Nobody wants to stay stuck. While it may be painful, confusing, or uncomfortable, courage is a friend who opens doors to a new life. Aligning with your intention instead of your fears will grow your confidence in knowing and pursuing what you want. Be afraid and show up anyway.

Now write your intention again here:

Remember, this is what we're going for. You can create anything you want by aligning with your future even when you're scared.

Born Worthy

Your worthiness is proven by your existence.
Your breathing. The beating of your heart.
Your mere presence is all that is needed to
establish your worth.
~Iyanla Vanzant

Most people know everyone is worthy of love and care and safety—everyone except yourself. It isn't easy for you to just start believing you're inherently worthy after decades of believing you aren't. After setting an intention, a pervasive sense of unworthiness can overshadow your ability to take actions to align with your intention.

Here's a conversation I have with my clients who believe they are unworthy.

>   ME: Do you believe babies are born worthy?

>   CLIENT: Yes, babies are born worthy.

>   ME: Are you sure? Every little baby?

>   CLIENT: Yes, of course they are.

>   ME: Every baby but you, right?

This simple inquiry illustrates how the logical mind tells us a basic truth, but the felt sense in the body believes there is one exception to worthiness.

When Life Gives You Lemons

I was sitting at my desk looking out the window while a client was sharing her painful feelings around believing she was unworthy of having what she wants in life. I heard her words while noticing a lemon tree in my neighbor's yard anchored in the dirt. Its branches were heavy with ripening fruit.

> I noticed the lemons were at different stages of development. Some of the lemons still had green on them while others had fallen to the ground soft with brown spots. I asked myself, *Which lemons are worthy? Is the green lemon unworthy? No, it's just in a maturing process and not ready to be picked. Is the rotting lemon on the ground unworthy? No, it's just lived its life and has let go of its attachment to the tree. The lemon no longer needs the tree's nourishment and is finding its way into the soil.*
>
> All lemons are worthy. To make the best lemonade, you might pick the lemons that are at the optimal stage of their development. The other lemons aren't *unworthy*, some just aren't ready to be harvested and others are past the stage of using them to make a refreshing drink with.

The same is true for all beings. We're all born inherently worthy. Inherently worthy means you cannot do anything to add to your worthiness. No success in this lifetime will make you more worthy than you inherently are. Likewise, nothing you do and nothing that happens to you can make you unworthy. If you're inherently worthy, then you *are* worthy. Period.

It's common for survivors of childhood trauma to believe they are unworthy, but that's just a belief—it's not true. It makes sense to think you're unworthy because of what happened to you, but to believe you're unworthy is to believe a lie.

Understanding that you're inherently worthy requires you to discern between what is true and what is not true. If you're ripe for healing from past abuse, then you'll do whatever is needed to grow beyond what happened to you. You'll challenge your thinking, you'll learn how to create a healthy future, and you'll get help as you need it. If you're unwilling to take the risks then you may never heal, but that doesn't mean you're unworthy—it just means you aren't ready.

Being inherently worthy does not mean you'll get everything you want. For example:

- Someone buying you something or not buying you something.
- Being offered a promotion at work or having a successful business.
- Owning a home or being able to easily provide for your family.

Your worthiness isn't connected to the good or bad things that happen in life. For example:

- Someone taking care of you or withholding what you need to survive or thrive.

- Someone you love living or dying.
- Whether others treat you well or abuse you.

Your worthiness isn't dependent on what you do or don't do. For example:

- Getting a summa cum laude award on your college diploma or failing your classes.
- Staying married or getting a divorce.
- Meeting someone's expectations or disappointing them.

Gap Work: I AM Inherently Worthy

Our worth is inherent, and therefore, is never on the negotiation table.
~J.S. Wolfe, The Unfolding: A Journey of Involution

Get out your journal and let's courageously challenge your thinking around being unworthy.

At the top of the page write: I AM inherently worthy.

Complete these sentences:

- What makes me believe I am unworthy is_____
- The ways I don't believe I'm worthy are_____
- The cost of not knowing my inherent worthiness is_____
- What stands in the way of knowing my worthiness is _____

Now, set all the doubts of your worthiness aside and connect with the part of you who knows everyone is born worthy. Take five minutes to write about the truth of your worthiness. Challenge everything you have believed up to this point. If you have difficulty, just imagine yourself as an innocent little baby and tell yourself what you would say to any other small child about *their* worthiness.

- The truth about my worthiness is that _____

Insecurity is different from truth. You're worthy *and* you can also feel unsure of whether you're worthy or not. If you feel insecure about your worthiness, you can rest in my confidence of your worthiness until you know for sure yourself.

Part Three
Living in The Gap

Your desire to change must be greater than your desire to stay the same.
~Colin Wilson

Living in The Gap is one way to free yourself from the ongoing impact of childhood sexual abuse. When you're living in The Gap, you'll practice everything you're learning in the space between Unconscious Incompetence (what you don't know how to change) and Conscious Competence (the new things you're doing to change your life).

- You'll learn to tell your story from a more sophisticated understanding and find true meaning about what happened in your past.
- You'll evolve from a wounded child with limited capacity to hold more than one idea at a time into an adult who has the capacity to hold a lot of complexity.
- You'll learn how to hold both the adult and child parts of yourself at the same time and will learn how to shift into the perspective of the adult and consciously respond instead of reacting to difficult circumstances.

You live in The Gap by **G**rounding yourself in **A**uthenticity and **P**resence. In this section you'll learn many ways to successfully navigate living in The Gap, including:

- Various barriers that get in the way of living in The Gap.
- How to have a healthy relationship with your feelings.
- The benefit of including and accepting all parts of yourself.
- Practice in setting appropriate boundaries.

- Owning your positive qualities.
- A deeper understanding of false beliefs and how to free yourself from them.

Authenticity

> *Authenticity is the daily practice of letting go of who we think we're supposed to be and embracing who we really are.*
> *~Brené Brown*

Inauthenticity is motivated by fear of rejection. Anxiety and distress about being rejected starts in early childhood when we start hiding parts of ourselves to avoid potential abandonment. For example, we learn to shut down sadness and turn up happiness. When we're kids, we shut down what's real to keep ourselves safe, but it's also inauthentic to pretend to feel happy when we're sad.

As a result of the paralyzing fear of rejection I felt, I changed who I was so people would like me. However, I never knew if the version of me people liked was actually me or the mask I wore. Most of the choices I made were an unconscious way of avoiding being discarded. My fears got worse in adulthood. I was afraid to share my opinions until everyone else shared theirs; I was afraid to disagree with anyone or to make a mistake. Nothing worked to alleviate my anxiety, and I felt abandoned and rejected even when people stayed in relationships with me.

In her iconic TED Talk, "The Power of Vulnerability," Brené Brown describes authenticity as a "daily practice of letting go of who we think we are supposed to be and embracing who we really are." I broke free from unhealthy relational dynamics only after I started showing up as my full authentic self. Talk about courage! While I felt super insecure in the beginning, grounding myself in authenticity and presence (The Gap) has been the most worthwhile choice I've ever made.

Presence

> *What you perceive as precious is not time but the one point that is out of time: the Now. That is precious indeed. The more you are focused on time—past and future—the more you miss the Now, the most precious thing there is.*
> *~Meister Eckhart*

You're present when you're aware of where you are in time and space. Being present means that you're mindful of whether you're feeling something that's happening now, or you're being triggered into an old feeling by a present situation. A lack of presence happens when you engage in automatic behaviors that come from unconscious thoughts and reactions to what's happening in the present moment. When you're not present, you'll react to your environment in unconscious habitual ways. A lack of presence will feel like a repetitive cycle in which you feel you have no power to change the outcome. When you're present, you'll respond to your environment in thoughtful ways that are appropriate for what's happening.

Being able to discern the difference between a reaction to the past and what's happening now will give you freedom to choose how to respond to what's happening in the present moment. For example, if you're having a flashback of the abuse, then it's the flashback happening now, not the abuse.

Barriers to Living in The Gap

The most authentic thing about us is our capacity to create, to overcome, to endure, to transform, to love, and to be greater than our suffering.
~Ben Okri

To ground yourself in authenticity and presence, you'll need to be aware of what gets in the way. In addition to the fear of rejection, some closely related barriers to living in The Gap are dissociation, codependency, and unconscious choices. Let's look at all three.

Dissociation

The problem with checking out so thoroughly is that it can leave us feeling dead inside, with little or no ability to feel our feelings in our bodies. The process of repair demands a re-association with the body, a commitment to dive into the body and feel today what we couldn't feel yesterday because it was too dangerous.
~Alexandra Katehakis, Mirror of Intimacy: Daily Reflections on Emotional and Erotic Intelligence

As a survival strategy, abuse survivors disconnect from their feelings and needs, and in some circumstances, they dissociate. Dissociation is an automatic coping mechanism that helps a person get through a traumatic event when it's happening. When a person dissociates, they disconnect from their body and the world around them. Where dissociating creates a level of safety when a trauma is happening, dissociating becomes problematic in adulthood and normal everyday life.

A person is generally unaware when they're dissociating and must learn how to keep themselves present by identifying the signs of dissociation. The most common sign of dissociating I experienced was losing my ability to answer questions during a perceived threat of rejection. I couldn't think clearly and would freeze; my throat would constrict making it impossible to speak. I also experienced flashbacks while being sexually intimate, which resulted in dissociating from my body, which was problematic in my relationships for many years.

Here's how you can tell if you're dissociating:

- Do you space out and/or enter a trance-like state, especially in times of stress?
- Do you feel detached from yourself, your emotions, and what's happening around you?
- Is there a lack of continuity between thoughts and ideas and actions?
- Do you have significant problems in relationships and/or other areas of life?
- Do you feel emotionally numb?

While mild dissociation doesn't necessarily interfere with daily living, severe dissociation can have a significant impact on the quality of your life. Dissociation impacts the ability to stay present, especially during conflict. Severe forms of dissociation could be a sign of a mental health problem. Seek an assessment from a therapist if you're concerned you may be experiencing any of the following:

- Post-traumatic stress disorder
- Clinical depression
- Schizophrenia
- Bipolar disorder
- Alcoholism or drug abuse
- Borderline personality disorder
- Suicidal ideation

If you tend to dissociate when there's no real threat to your safety, you can learn how to keep yourself in the present moment. The remedy for dissociation is staying connected to your body and staying in the present moment.

Here are some practices to help you stay present:

- Open your eyes and keep your attention on your surroundings. Notice what you're seeing, smelling, hearing, and tasting and name what you're aware of in your environment.
- Breathe. Stay connected and aware of your breath and breathe slowly and deeply. You could tell yourself, "I'm okay. I'm safe right now."

- Practice staying connected to your body by keeping some of your awareness on feeling your feet on the ground.

Gap Work: Staying in Your Body

*All art is a kind of confession, more or less oblique.
All artists, if they are to survive, are forced, at last,
to tell the whole story; to vomit the anguish up.*
~James Baldwin

Let's practice connecting with your body.

When you stay out of your thinking mind and in the felt sense in your body, feelings you've resisted in the past can move through you with a few focused deep breaths. Feelings can come in scary waves when connected to words, but when you allow feelings to simply be there, they move naturally and organically in a short period of time.

In this exercise you'll stay in your body and feel whatever is happening as simple sensations without adding a story to any feelings you're having.

Try this practice the next time you have a difficult feeling arise or feel disconnected from your body.

1. With your eyes open, draw a slow breath to the count of four down into your belly.
2. Exhale to the count of four keeping your attention fully on your exhale.
3. Continue to breathe in this way for several breaths keeping all your attention on the movement of your breath. Focus your attention on the rise and fall of your belly.
4. Whenever you notice a dialogue starting in your head, simply come back to your breath. If you find it difficult to stop thinking, repeat the words, "Right now, I'm here and I'm okay."
5. Repeat several times until the feeling has passed.
6. Take a few notes in your journal to track your experience of this exercise.

As you focus on the sensations in your body (instead of the words you hear), the sensations in your body will rise and fall and move through you with very little impact. You can use this practice several times throughout the day, and you can also use it to stay present all day long. You may need to remind yourself many times throughout the day to breathe. As soon as you notice you've lost presence, then come back to being aware of your body and your breath.

You can do this exercise with your eyes closed or open, whichever is needed to bring you into your body. You can use all your senses to stay connected to your body. Here are some ideas:

- Name what is in your environment. See if you can name what you're seeing and hearing. Notice if there are birds chirping and the direction the sound is coming from.
- Notice if there's a breeze in the air. Is it warm or cool? Can you feel your hair moving in the breeze?
- Feel your feet on the ground.
- Rub your finger and thumb together and notice the ridges which make up your fingerprints.
- Clap your hands together and say out loud: "I'm here."
- Keep part of your attention on your breath.
- Be aware of your thoughts instead of unconsciously giving them power.
- Set a timer to check in with your body every hour.

Noticing what's happening in your body will become one of your greatest tools of discernment. Staying in your body and connected with yourself is a practice which leads to increased awareness and access to the wisdom your body has for you. With practice and consistency, you'll be able to use your body as a finely tuned instrument to guide you through every choice you make. Practice staying in your body throughout the day.

Codependence

> *So then, the relationship of self to other is the complete realization that loving yourself is impossible without loving everything defined as other than yourself.*
> ~Alan Watts

In its simplest form, codependence is a relational pattern where a person is disconnected from their own feelings and needs and takes on being overly responsible for meeting the feelings and needs of other people.

People who were abused as children often create codependent relationships from a deep fear of abandonment. My unconscious codependent behaviors were an attempt to avoid the possibility of anyone ever leaving me, and it came with a huge cost—I lost connection with myself.

Gap Work: Codependent Behaviors

I used to spend so much time reacting and responding to everyone else that my life had no direction. Other people's lives, problems, and wants set the course for my life.
Once I realized it was okay for me to think about and identify what I wanted, remarkable things began to take place in my life.
~Melody Beattie

I had all the following codependent behaviors. Circle the codependent behaviors you experience.

- I have a difficult time making decisions in relationships.
- I habitually defer to others.
- I say yes to requests without considering myself.
- I let what matters to others take priority over what matters to me.
- I ask others what they think while not sharing (or knowing) what I think.
- I'm agreeable to avoid abandonment or rejection.
- I feel dissatisfied in my relationship but I'm doing nothing to change it.
- I have unspoken expectations.
- I feel compelled to do things for others which they can do for themselves.
- I'm chronically disappointed when others don't show up the way I want them to.
- I easily know what others feel but have difficulty knowing what I feel.
- To get approval I overwork, over-give, over-do, and over-love.
- I support others' dreams and give up on my own.
- I take on more than I want to or feel capable of taking on.

Get out your journal make a list of any other ways you're disconnected from your authenticity and presence by being codependent. You don't have to know how to change codependent behaviors right now, you just need to write down what you know needs to change.

Remember that you must give up codependence to live authentically. Take a few minutes to write down some of the codependent behaviors you've already stopped doing or are in the process of letting go of.

- What changes have I already made?
- In what ways am I making choices that are right for me?
- What boundaries am I already setting?

Let's take another step and dig deep to bring awareness (presence) to any unconscious choices you're currently making. You can add to this list over time as you become more aware of the choices you're making.

Unconscious Choices

> *You know how sometimes you tell yourself that you have a choice, but really you don't have a choice? Just because there are alternatives doesn't mean they apply to you.*
> *~Rick Yancey,* The 5th Wave

Becoming authentic isn't easy; you must bring awareness to the unconscious choices you make, then make new conscious choices. Here are some of the unconscious and inauthentic choices I made.

- I pursued an early education teaching career to get my mother's approval.
    Even though I'm inherently a teacher, early education wasn't authentic to me. I now teach through my coaching career.

- I quit classes when I didn't get the best grade.
    This choice was made from a fear of believing I wasn't good enough and needing to hide that from others. I now do my best and consider myself a lifelong learner.

- I made myself into a chameleon to fit in.
    I did what everyone else was doing so I wouldn't be rejected. I now embrace my unique way of being and thinking.

- I constantly asked what other people thought so I didn't have to take responsibility for making a wrong choice.

    I didn't take the time to know what I really thought and wouldn't take the risk to let people know. I have now taken the time to know what I want and often share spontaneously.

- I drank alcohol to avoid feeling shame over what happened to me.

    Instead of being authentically with my pain, I pushed it away. I now feel what I feel without grasping or avoiding.

- I had sex when I didn't want to with people who didn't care about me.

    It was inauthentic to share my body with someone who didn't honor my sacredness. I now only share in ways that are authentic for me.

Let's look at the choices you're making that are inauthentic.

Gap Work: Inauthentic Choices

Only the truth of who you are, if realized, will set you free.
~Eckhart Tolle

Get out your journal.

Maybe you're conscious of the choices you're making that aren't right for you, or maybe you aren't fully aware of them yet. That's okay. You'll become more authentic one choice at a time. The first step is to find what's authentic for you. Start by answering the following questions:

- What am I currently doing that I don't want to do?
- What am I not doing that I really want to?

Authenticity depends on you to:

- Take the time to know yourself and what matters most to you.
- Learn how to share what matters to you with others in honest and responsible ways.
- Take actions which are right for you even if others disapprove.

Look at your list and choose one change you're willing to make to start being authentic. Write that here and in your journal.

Healthy Relationship with Your Feelings

Anything that's human is mentionable, and anything that is mentionable can be more manageable. When we can talk about our feelings, they become less overwhelming, less upsetting, and less scary.
~Fred Rogers

When we're connected to—and understand—our feelings they'll become a source of wisdom. Knowing what you're feeling in the moment takes time. Being able to name your feelings without identifying as your feelings is a skill that can be learned. The more connected you are to your feelings, the more you can use them as a tuning fork to know if you're on the right path or not.

Feelings can act as an early warning system guiding us toward safety, but childhood sexual abuse survivors lose access to their inner guidance system, and everything can feel like a threat. If we don't learn how to use our feelings in healthy ways, then our feelings can leave us in turmoil. Feelings can go on overdrive, leaving one feeling unsafe even when there's no eminent danger. Or feelings can be muted, making someone unaware of dangerous situations they should be paying attention to.

Our emotional world starts developing in early childhood. When abuse is present, we tend to become disconnected from our feelings and over time our internal navigation system stops working. When you become disconnected from your feelings, you can't have a healthy relationship with yourself or other people. One way to know if you're disconnected from your feelings is if, instead of being able to name your feelings, you habitually react instead of consciously respond to situations and circumstances.

The following list includes ways you can know you're reacting to your early wounding:

- Emotional outbursts.
- Difficulty dealing with conflict.

- Addiction to drugs or alcohol.
- Depression and suicide ideation.
- Pervasive sense of feeling alone.
- Feeling misunderstood most of the time.
- Feeling disconnected from yourself.
- Passive-aggressive behavior.
- Being stuck in the same experiences and the same old story.
- Projecting emotions onto others.
- Acting emotions out in destructive ways.
- Dissociating.

Having a healthy relationship with yourself requires getting connected to your feelings in healthy ways. Once you're able to name your feelings, you can learn how to use them to determine if you're truly in danger or if you're just stretching out of your comfort zone and just feeling scared.

Nonviolent Communication

> *Communication is a skill that you can learn. It's like riding a bicycle or typing. If you're willing to work at it, you can rapidly improve the quality of every part of your life.*
> *~Brian Tracy*

Nonviolent Communication (NVC), a concept created by psychologist Marshall Rosenburg, is based on principles of nonviolence and helps people develop a healthy relationship with their feelings and needs. NVC offers classes and trainings on how to communicate in healthy and responsible ways and naming your feelings is key to having a healthy relationship with them.

Gap Work: Naming Your Feelings

> *If you're going to make an emotional connection with somebody, whether it's in the story or in the world, there's a certain amount of self-acceptance that is required.*
> *~George Saunders*

The purpose of this practice is to cultivate your capacity to be with all your feelings. Work with them at your own pace and eventually you will be able to tolerate big feelings without collapsing into despair.

We have many more feelings than the six commonly known basic emotions including sadness, happiness, fear, anger, surprise, and disgust. Below is a list of some feelings we all have:

happy	playful	jubilant	warmhearted
peaceful	disappointed	annoyed	hopeful
amused	isolated	guilty	triumphant
delighted	jealous	pleased	lonely
confused	tender	regretful	inadequate
gloomy	compassionate	disheartened	thankful
shameful	grateful	terrified	enraged
optimistic	insecure	anxious	enthusiastic

You can get connected to yourself through a simple practice of asking yourself what you're feeling throughout the day. If you're like me, having been abused made it difficult for me to name even my most basic feelings. In the beginning of my healing process, I found having a list of feelings to choose from made it easier for me to connect with them. You can find many lists of feelings online, but you can go to LeilaReyes.com/FreedomfromShame to download some of my favorites. Print one out so you can review it often.

Making Room for Feelings

Feelings demand living space.
~Isidore Isou

It's understandable to want to push away difficult emotions, but remember, nobody has ever died from feeling their feelings. If you let them, feelings will simply come and go making it possible for you to live more fully. Include what you normally hide or distance yourself from and discover you can create healthy love and connection by simply being present to what you're authentically feeling.

Once you can name your feelings, processing your emotions will be a valuable part of creating a healthy relationship with yourself. Naming your feelings and processing your emotions feed each other. Processing your emotions is a therapeutic process where you delve into your feelings either verbally or somatically. As you process your emotions, you'll then be able to name your feelings with growing confidence.

Of course, to heal your relationship with yourself and others, you'll need to also learn how to refrain from habitual reactions and start responding in healthy ways. Over-processing feelings can turn into an unhealthy habit instead of an effective tool used to deepen understanding. The Buddhist parable below of two monks and a woman illustrates the difference between healthy and unhealthy processing.

> Two Monks and a Woman
>
> A senior and junior monk were traveling together. They came to a river and saw a beautiful young woman also wanting to cross the river. She asked if they could help her cross to the other side.
>
> The two monks had taken vows to not touch a woman, but the older monk immediately offered to help. He carried her across the river, set her down, and the two monks continued on their way.
>
> The younger monk was visibly upset the older monk had carried the woman across the river. An hour passed without a word between them as they continued their journey.
>
> Two more hours passed, then three. Finally, the younger monk blurted out, "As monks, we are not permitted to touch a woman. Why then would you carry the woman across the river?"
>
> The older monk looked at him and replied, "Brother, I set her down on the other side of the river. Why are you still carrying her?"

It's important to be connected to, and understand, all your feelings, not just the good ones. Your feelings are your feelings, and you don't need to justify them or give a reason for feeling what you feel. It's your birthright to feel the way you do without judgment. Adding meaning to what you're feeling hurts you more. The meaning may or may not be accurate, but adding meaning takes us away from being present and deeper into additional painful feelings.

For example, if a friend doesn't call you when they say they will, don't add the meaning they don't care—that will hurt more. Instead of making up a story, ask them directly and make agreements going forward. If they don't keep the agreements they make with you, then maybe they don't care. Most importantly, don't interpret someone not caring to mean you don't deserve to be cared for.

Do your best to refrain from adding meaning to your feelings—just feel them—without any judgment. Here are some common feelings we all have:

- I feel angry.
- I feel sad.
- I feel unloved.

Resist the temptation to add "because" after you name a feeling. For example:

- I feel angry *because* you never do what you say you will do.
- I feel sad *because* nobody cares about me.
- I feel unloved *because* my parents got divorced.

Gap Work: A Part of Me Feels...

The most terrifying thing is to accept oneself completely.
~C.G. Jung

Internal Family Systems (IFS), created by Dr. Richard Schwartz, is an evidence-based therapeutic model that helps to understand and organize all parts of the individual self. For example, you have a part of you that's sad and a part that's happy. It would be more beneficial to acknowledge the part of you that's sad than to push that part away and force the happy part to show up.

Wanting to avoid "bad" feelings is understandable, but telling yourself you're happy when you're not only solidifies the feeling you're trying to get away from. A common misunderstanding is believing if you let yourself feel the "bad" feelings then they'll consume you. Saying "I AM happy" when you're sad creates a mis-attunement between your inner and outer experience. If you try to stop your feelings, that's when they become overwhelming scary monsters that must be avoided at all costs.

A more effective use of "I AM" would be to simply include everything as *part of your experience*, which is constantly shifting and nothing to be afraid of.

Saying "I AM..." is one of the most powerful manifestation techniques human beings can use. The phrase "I AM" connects you to your higher self and is a spiritual way of saying you're one with the Divine. Using "I AM" is a process which allows you to create at the level of your identity, so it's important to be conscious of how you're using this technique.

Instead of trying to overpower your sadness by being happy when you're feeling sad, simply acknowledge the sadness (or any other feelings) as part of your experience, like this:

First say, "I AM sad" and notice how sadness seems to take over your entire experience leaving no room for any other feeling or experience.

Take a moment to really feel this in your body.

Now say, "A part of me is feeling sad." With an emphasis on *a part of me*.

Notice how it feels better. Even if you feel just a little better.

Saying "I AM sad" is a way of *becoming* the sadness. Saying "A part of me is feeling sad" is a way of disidentifying with the sadness and including sadness as part of your very human experience.

Acknowledging how a part of you is feeling is what allows feelings to pass through you instead of getting stuck. Including all parts of yourself gives you access to more of yourself and is quite honoring of painful experiences you had earlier in life while not letting them take over in current time.

The "A part of me feels" exercise is one step of a practice given to me by my spiritual teacher, Jennifer Welwood. I have found that using the tool "A part of me is feeling _____" has the power to instantly alleviate suffering. Try it and see for yourself.

- Remember, becoming aware of what you're doing is the key to changing your experience. Check it out for yourself. Over the next two weeks use the language "A part of me feels..."
- Catch yourself if you try to get away from a feeling and acknowledge the feeling by saying, "A part of me feels..."

Journal about what you notice.

- How often do you catch yourself avoiding difficult feelings?
- What do you notice when you use "A part of me feels..."?
- What is shifting and changing as you use this technique?

Self-Acceptance

Bring your whole self to the experience. Because the more you do that, the more people get to see that, the more comfortable everybody's gonna be with it.
~Bozoma Saint John

People who experience childhood trauma abandon their authenticity to create safety. Self-rejection was a brilliant strategy at the time of the abuse, but later in life safety is found in self-acceptance, where you're connected to all parts of yourself. Let's take a step toward accepting all parts of who you are.

Gap Work: The Parts We Reject

Because true belonging only happens when we present our authentic, imperfect selves to the world, our sense of belonging can never be greater than our level of self-acceptance.
~Brené Brown, Daring Greatly

In this exercise, you'll list the human qualities you don't want anyone to know you have. Circle the qualities you judge others as having and the qualities you never want to be called.

Abusive	Coward	Foolish
Arrogant	Cruel	Frivolous
Apathetic	Defensive	Gossiper
Bitch	Devious	Gullible
Childish	Evil	Hostile
Controlling	Flaky	Hypocritical

Ignorant	Melodramatic	Selfish
Impatient	Nag	Sleazy
Impulsive	Needy	Spoiled
Insecure	Nosy	Stubborn
Insignificant	Oversensitive	Stupid
Irrational	Perfectionist	Uncaring
Irresponsible	Pessimist	Uncooperative
Jealous	Possessive	Unethical
Judgmental	Pushy	Ungrateful
Know-it-all	Rebellious	Vain
Lazy	Reckless	Violent
Liar	Resentful	Whiny
Manipulative	Rude	
Mean	Self-indulgent	

Now, take about ten minutes to journal what you notice.

It wasn't easy for me to make a list of qualities I pushed away. I believed if I had those "bad" qualities it would mean I was bad. I would have been filled with shame if someone called me uncaring, mean, heartless, or selfish, so be kind and gentle with yourself completing this exercise. Remember, these are just human qualities that everyone has.

Being Human

> *Being human is being a lot of things*
> *at the same time.*
> *~Matthias Schoenaerts*

Because the qualities on the previous pages are human qualities, it means we all have them—every single one. We don't express all human qualities at the same time or to the same degree or even to the same people, and we learn to hide qualities we believe are undesirable. When we reject our human qualities, we separate ourselves from others.

It's impossible to be authentic when we're rejecting ourselves.

Here's an example using the quality "mean", which is a human quality. Young girls are socialized to be nice even when it's not in their best interest, like during sexual abuse. Unfortunately, we then grow up being nice to everyone but ourselves and express our "meanness" internally.

You can tell you're rejecting a human quality if you're upset when someone judges you or if you do everything in your power to not let anyone think you have a particular quality.

In the past if someone called me "mean" I would have been horrified. Because I couldn't let anyone think I was mean I was an easy target for being taken advantage of. I would be nice even when it meant putting myself in danger. Being nice when it wasn't good for me made me untrustworthy to myself. It was difficult to admit that I was showing up in relationships in ways to avoid losing love and connection, but nothing changed until I took the risk to be right where I am—mess and all. In the beginning, it's not easy showing up as your authentic self but stick with it and you will find your way to authentic presence.

A sign you're ready for transformation is when you're willing to be honest with yourself and others and be right where you are. Here are some common signs that show you're ready to transform your life:

- Being willing to be vulnerable with yourself and others around what isn't working.
- Being willing to ask for help.
- Having the courage to see yourself as you are and as you aren't.

Being grounded in authentic presence is being authentic no matter what "real" looks like. You've taken some powerful steps to reveal what's true right now. Let's take another step by taking an honest look at yourself, *without being hard on yourself,* if you see something you don't like.

Gap Work: Self-Acceptance Assessment

How you love yourself is how you teach others to love you.
~Rupi Kaur

An effective way to evaluate your self-acceptance is whether your inner and outer worlds match. Place a check mark by each answer you feel is true about yourself most of the time.

[ ] My inner world matches my outer experience.

In the past, I was happy on the outside while I suffered with deep insecurity on the inside. I did everything I could to hide my insecurity and show up as a confident, capable woman.

Today, sometimes I feel confident and sometimes insecure: when I feel insecure, I let those close to me know so I don't suffer alone.

[ ] I only say yes to what I truly want to say yes to.

In the past, I said yes to the point of exhausting myself and having no energy left to do what I wanted for myself.

[ ] People respect my boundaries and rarely cross them.

In the past, I felt angry and resentful. I didn't understand why people didn't know what I needed from them, even though I never told them. (Not telling others directly what you need but expecting them to guess is a sign of codependence.)

[ ] People know how I truly feel about things.

In the past, I didn't know how I felt about things, so I *couldn't* let others know. In the past, I hid how I felt hurt and rejected when people didn't read my mind.

[ ] I share my opinions even if they're different from what other people think.

In the past, I always shared last so I could adapt myself to the group.

[ ] I never over-give and let people know I need reciprocity before giving more.

In the past, I gave and pushed away anything coming my way. Then I felt used and taken advantage of.

[ ] I know what I want and need and let others know in ways that make it easy for them to understand.

In the past, I was completely disconnected from my own needs. If I knew what I needed, I communicated in angry, resentful ways.

[ ] I don't worry about disappointing others.

In the past, I took responsibility for how others experienced me and avoided doing anything I thought would disappoint them.

Problematic Behaviors

> *It is by going down into the abyss that we recover the treasures of life. Where you stumble, there lies your treasure. The very cave you are afraid to enter turns out to be the source of what you are looking for.*
> *~ Joseph Campbell*

When I started my journey, I couldn't have checked any of the self-acceptance boxes. I found self-honesty was difficult, but meant I was ready for transformation.

Like many survivors of sexual abuse, I was a proud helper. I loved helping others whether it was standing at the sink when I was a kid washing dishes with my grandmother or cleaning up in the kitchen far into adulthood. However, I missed many parties because I was too busy making myself useful by cleaning up after everyone.

Through therapy and being willing to be honest with myself, I discovered helping was not completely authentic. I believed my value was in doing what I could for someone else. If I wasn't helping, I was useless.

My compulsion to help was mostly unconscious. I never considered if I had the time or energy to help, or if I even *wanted* to help. At the time, I believed my desire was to make it easy on everyone else so they could have a good time. I have since discovered helping was mostly a way to help me feel like I mattered. I helped, and helped, and helped. I helped regardless of whether my help was needed or wanted.

The pattern was so strong that for years I had to check in with myself to make sure I wasn't helping just to prove I matter.

Being a helper isn't bad. There's just no choice when we engage in unconscious patterns. If there's no choice, then there can be no authenticity. Helping wasn't the problem for me. The problem was in *believing I didn't matter unless I was helping.*

Once I became aware my "helpful" behavior was motivated by a harmful belief, then I knew what I needed to know to stop the unconscious behavior. Instead of automatically stepping in to help, I now take time to check in with myself to see if I want to help or not. I also check in with the person I want to help to see if my help is needed or wanted by them. If my help is not needed, I don't take it personally to mean I don't matter. Today, I'm conscious of when, how, and why I'm helping and have since discovered authentic ways I enjoy helping others. And I really enjoy myself at parties whether I'm helping or not.

Let's look at what behaviors might get in the way of your healing.

Gap Work: Problematic Behaviors

We cannot change anything until we accept it.
Condemnation does not liberate, it oppresses.
~Carl Jung

Get out your journal and ask yourself the following questions:
- What are the unconscious ways I show up with people?
- Where do I feel I have no choice?
- What behavior do I most want to stop, but feel powerless to change?
- What do I feel is not my responsibility, but I keep doing it?

To practice stopping automatic behaviors, check in with yourself first. For example, if helping is one of your automatic behaviors, then try this:

Instead of automatically helping, take the time to check in with yourself. Stop. Put your hand on your heart and ask yourself one of these questions:
- Do I want to help in this situation?
- Is my help necessary?
- Is my help wanted?
- Has my help been asked for?

Practice these new responses in place of your auto-response to help:
- When someone asks for your help, tell them, "Let me think about it and get back to you."
- If you want to make sure you can schedule in your offer to help before committing to helping say, "I don't have my schedule with me. I'll check it and get back to you."
- If you don't want to help, say, "No, I'm not available to help with that."

The key to self-acceptance and showing up with authentic presence is to first become aware of your unconscious patterns, then to consciously stop doing them. In the example of helping, you must stop the unconscious habit of saying yes without checking in with yourself first.

Even if you know you want to say yes, practice taking some "cool off" time to seriously consider your other commitments and whether saying yes is the right choice for you. Sometimes you'll want to say yes but doing so wouldn't be good for you. In that situation say, "I'd really love to, but I have other commitments and won't be able to help you." If you feel inauthentic about saying you have other commitments, remind yourself the commitment you're making is to be true to yourself.

Once you stop yourself from automatic behaviors, you're on your way to living authentically. Remember, creating new responses takes time, practice, and patience with yourself.

Now let's look at how setting boundaries is essential to living in The Gap.

Boundaries

*Whatever you're willing to put up with is exactly
what you'll get.*
~Anonymous

A boundary is simply a limit you set for what you will and will not accept from yourself or others. Boundaries are first taught by early caregivers when it was their responsibility to model setting boundaries. In abuse situations where healthy boundaries were non-existent, it would have been dangerous for a young person to attempt setting boundaries with their caregivers. Freezing is often the safest response a child can make when abuse is happening. In contrast, not knowing how to set appropriate boundaries in your adult life will either create a lack of safety for yourself or put up a wall that prevents closeness and intimacy from happening.

The ability to discern between healthy and unhealthy boundaries will be compromised if you've been abused as a child. The child whose physical boundaries are crossed becomes confused around what's healthy and safe and may grow up believing unhealthy boundaries are normal. Survivors of childhood sexual abuse tend to grow up unintentionally putting themselves in dangerous or unsafe situations. I put myself in many dangerous situations before learning how to set healthy boundaries.

> I was forty years old and still didn't know how to stop someone invading my personal space. I was with a group of friends at a mountain resort for a weekend gathering. There were more people than our group in a large community hot tub. I knew most people in our group but not everyone.
>
> Our group was in the large hot tub huddled in a circle. We were talking quietly with each other when a man I didn't know included himself in our circle. I assumed he knew someone in our group, but I didn't know for sure. He moved closer to me and the hairs on the back

of my neck stood up. Although I was shaking inside, externally I was frozen.

Eventually, this man was standing right next to me in the water. I was paralyzed, unable to move away or tell him to not come any closer. I could barely breathe. I pretended he wasn't there and when he put his arm around me, I didn't move. He pulled me closer, and I held my breath.

The "freeze" trauma response, discussed earlier, was activated as soon as this man entered the water—even before he joined our circle. *My body told me he wasn't safe*, but because I didn't know how to set a boundary I couldn't move when he got closer to me. It was a friend in our circle that noticed I needed help and rescued me. I was safe but only because someone else was tuned into what was happening.

Getting Familiar With Boundaries

> *The boundary to what we can accept is the boundary to our freedom.*
> *~Tara Brach*

As an adult, the ability to set boundaries is an important part of creating well-being in present time. Learning how to set healthy boundaries will be a game changer around self-esteem and leads to personal safety. An important step in setting healthy boundaries is understanding where boundaries need to be set. Some important areas to consider are:

- Boundaries around your time.
- Boundaries around work responsibilities.
- Boundaries with people.

Time Boundaries

> *"No" is a complete sentence.*
> *~Anonymous*

One of our most precious commodities is our time. You'll know you need to set time boundaries if you're doing things for other people, but never seem to get to do things for yourself.

People who don't have clear time boundaries tend to prioritize doing things for others over taking time for themselves. While they say they want to exercise regularly, take a vacation, or even read a book, they instead wear themselves out meeting other people's demands leaving no time to tend to their own desires.

Work Boundaries

> *Lack of boundaries invites lack of respect.*
> *~Anonymous*

An area where you might feel particularly out of balance is at work. You'll know your self-care suffers if you're feeling exhausted instead of enlivened by your contribution.

People who don't set appropriate boundaries at work:

- Take on extra responsibility at work without getting compensated.
- Feel obligated to take on extra work nobody else wants to do.
- Are the last one to leave work.
- Feel unseen, underappreciated, and unacknowledged for the extra work they do.
- Work in a position they don't want to be working in.

People Boundaries

> *Being honest might not get you a lot of friends, but*
> *it will get you the right ones.*
> *~John Lennon*

Fear of rejection, retaliation, or abandonment gets in the way of most survivors of childhood abuse being able to set clear boundaries as adults.

You'll know you need to set boundaries with others if you:

- Feel diminished by how you're being treated.
- Have difficulty speaking up and advocating for what you want.
- Habitually feel unseen and unheard.

Knowing how to set boundaries that inspire people to honor them is an essential skill you can learn. It took effort to stop blaming myself for how people hurt me. It took even more effort to see that I was creating my own lack of safety by not learning how to set boundaries around my physical space. I reminded myself that there are no reasons or justifications that could ever make me responsible for someone hurting me. I reminded myself that it's *never* the child's responsibility to set boundaries to create safety—that was the adult's job. Nobody taught me healthy boundaries, but once I was an adult, it was my responsibility to teach myself.

The people who respect your boundaries are the people who will appreciate knowing what they need to do to stay in relationship with you. The risk in setting boundaries is that you'll find there are people in your life who can't or won't respect them. Once you're aware of the people not respecting your boundaries, you may no longer be able to tolerate them being in your life. Or you may decide to limit time with people who don't respect your boundaries.

There's great benefit in taking risks to set boundaries. Letting go of people who can't or won't respect your boundaries will make room for people who can. You may feel sad ending relationships that have been important to you, but it can also be exciting to finally have the tools to create the kinds of relationships you want. The people who respect your boundaries are the people who will appreciate knowing what they need to do to stay in relationship with you.

Setting boundaries can be terrifying to the hurt part of us, but having clear boundaries with ourselves and others is the only way to have healthy relationships and create true safety. A healthy boundary is not rigid or loose, but appropriate for the situation. The good news is if you don't know how to set healthy boundaries, you can learn. Learning how to set healthy boundaries can feel awkward in the beginning and it takes courage to implement and stick with them, but with practice and consistency it will become easier.

Now let's set some boundaries.

Gap Work: Setting Boundaries

When you say "yes" to others, make sure you're not saying "no" to yourself.
~Paulo Coelho

Get out your journal. This exercise may take up to a week but start with setting aside thirty minutes to work through this exercise and then decide if you need more time.

Consider every area of your life. Identify what you're doing that you don't really want to. Feelings of anger, resentment, or frustration are clues of saying yes when you want to say no.

- What are you saying "Yes" to which you don't want to?
- Where do you feel manipulated into doing something you don't want to?
- What situations do you feel victimized or bullied into saying yes in?
- Who or what are you afraid of saying "No" to?

Consider how you spend your time.

- In what ways are you giving your time to others, but not having enough for yourself?
- If you had all the time in the world, what would you choose to do with your time? What would you make a priority?
- Does self-care take a backseat to other people's needs?

Consider your work environment.

- Are you working more than you're compensated for?
- In what ways do you feel compelled to work more than others?
- Does the hope for appreciation when you over-commit get in the way of saying no?

Consider your relationships.

- Do you agree to do things you really don't want to do?
- Do you give away possessions (including money) at your own expense?
- Do you have sex when you don't want to?

Knowing how you feel will help you understand what boundaries need to be set. Write uncensored, like a stream of consciousness. This is for your eyes only. No judgment. Imagine giving your thoughts, and anything swirling around in your head, to the pen. Don't stop to read or edit what you're writing.

Include the insights you now have around boundaries as you journal about the following.

- I feel resentful when...
- I am disappointed when...
- I don't like it when...
- I find it hard to say no when...

Look at everything you just wrote. Feeling disappointed, angry, or resentful toward yourself or another person are clues that a boundary could be set. These boundaries may be with yourself or others. Use everything you just discovered and make a list of boundaries you would like to set.

Here are some examples:

1. I prioritize my self-care.

Prioritizing your self-care includes protecting the time you need for exercise, getting enough sleep, and regular meals. A specific boundary may include not working late, getting to sleep at a consistent hour, or walking during your break instead of working through lunch.

One way that makes it easier to set boundaries around your time is to add yourself to your own calendar. I call this a sacred appointment. This is how it works:

Schedule an appointment with yourself to cook dinner at 5:30pm. If someone asks you to stay late at work, simply say, "I'm sorry, I have an appointment tonight and won't be able to." You don't need to explain your sacred appointments to *anyone*. Taking back your schedule will give you the energy and flexibility to invest time, energy, and resources in yourself and what you most want to do with your life. It's your life and nobody is going to prioritize your life for you—that's your responsibility. And, you're not obligated to reveal that your commitment is to your own self-care.

2. I say "No" when I don't want to do something.

Telling people "No" can be difficult for abuse survivors. Taking your power back from an earlier sense of powerlessness requires that you learn how to say no. A specific boundary around saying "No" may include only having sex when you truly want to, not going to an event you aren't interested in, or—my personal favorite—not letting someone invade your personal space.

3. I only spend time with people who value my time.

I was the perfect doormat. I accommodated myself to everyone's changing schedule. I was always on time myself and waited longer than I wanted to. I let people cancel on me with no consequence and when they arrived late to a meeting I would lie and say it didn't bother me. The result was a festering resentment and a sense that I didn't matter. Setting a boundary in this situation requires communication.

Here are some things you could say to set this boundary:

- I feel angry when you're late for lunch and I'd like you to be on time in the future. Will you agree to being on time?
- I notice I feel irritated when you consistently arrive late for our meeting. I don't enjoy waiting for you to arrive. Please give me a call when you're leaving your home so I can time my arrival closer to when you will get there.
- I set aside one hour for lunch. If you're late, I'm going to order my lunch and start eating without you so I'm not late for my next appointment.
- I value my time and yours so I'm on time for our lunch date. When you're consistently late, it tells me you're not making our meeting a priority. If you're late again for your lunch, then I'm not going to meet you for lunch again.

Review what you've discovered and identify one boundary you're willing to practice setting here:

The boundary I am willing to set is:

Feeling uncomfortable with setting boundaries is common if you haven't had practice. Take a few minutes to write out what you imagine will happen when you set this boundary.

If I set this boundary, then:

Let any fears come up, but don't let them stop you from moving forward. Here are some considerations in making a plan to set your boundary:

- Decide how you'll communicate your boundary.
- Decide what you'll do to keep the boundary and what will happen if the other person doesn't respect it.
- Set a date to communicate your boundary.
- Practice having the conversation with a coach or support person.

At this stage, simply getting comfortable with setting your boundary is what's most important. It can be helpful to practice setting a boundary out loud. Using a mirror to practice what you want to say or practicing with a friend can make setting a boundary easier.

My plan for setting a boundary is:

Now that you have a plan for setting your boundary, take about five minutes to write about your experience. Notice what you're feeling. Are you feeling anxious or excited? Also, imagine how you would feel if others were honoring this boundary.

As I learned how to set healthy boundaries, the way I felt about myself changed. As the way I felt about myself changed, my ability to set healthy boundaries increased. The result is a sense of my increased capacity to create safety for myself wherever I go. Setting a boundary for the first time doesn't always go smoothly, but if you're clear and consistent in setting a boundary, you'll get good at it.

Keep in mind that setting boundaries creates safety for you and the other person. Letting others know what your boundaries are will help them know what's important to you. Whether they respect your boundaries or not, you'll get valuable feedback from their response.

Here are some red flags to watch for as you practice setting boundaries:

- Discounting or minimizing your boundary. They might call you too sensitive.
- Redirecting blame. They might point out the one time you were late.
- Defending themselves. They might say they couldn't make it on time because of traffic or getting a last-minute phone call.
- Feeling victimized. They might get angry at you for not understanding how busy they are.
- Disappearing. They might avoid you in the future.

Learning how to set boundaries can be very difficult, but it will be worth the effort. Setting boundaries demands being willing to let go. People who don't respect your boundaries once you've communicated them and given them a fair chance to honor them may be people you choose to no longer have in your life. With practice, you'll eventually set boundaries without the fear of retaliation or abandonment, even if relationships end.

Positive Qualities

You are the sum total of everything you've ever seen, heard, eaten, smelled, been told, forgot—it's all there.
~Maya Angelou

As a survivor of childhood trauma, you've likely developed many positive qualities because of what you lived through. Your best qualities often start as compensation for the wounding you experienced. My helpful quality developed to compensate for feeling unworthy or unloved and to avoid being judged or rejected by others.

Compensatory qualities are used to prevent some perceived negative experiences from happening. For example, you may become fiercely independent to avoid having to rely on anyone. While independence is a wonderful quality, when it's expressed in reaction to a wound, independence becomes a barrier to getting the support and connection you really need. The healthiest expression of independence, therefore, is to consciously choose when to take care of things on your own and when to rely on others.

Common compensatory qualities include:

- Becoming super independent so you don't have to rely on anyone but yourself.
   The cost of this quality is feeling alone and overwhelmed.

- Over-accommodating so someone doesn't think you're selfish.
   The cost of this quality is never having your needs considered, then feeling angry and resentful of never being considered.

- Being super helpful and making yourself indispensable to avoid being abandoned.
   The cost of this quality is feeling taken advantage of and never feeling like an equal.

In addition to being a great helper, a compensatory quality I developed was tolerance. I was good at tolerating bad behavior and accepting less than what I wanted.

I was able to tolerate being uncomfortable in my body to make others comfortable and give them what I believed they wanted.

Gap Work: Positive Qualities

Inner peace doesn't come from getting what we want, but from remembering who we are.
~Marianne Williamson

Get out your journal.

Each positive quality can get in the way of your authenticity when you're using the quality to avoid something like rejection. Becoming aware of compensatory qualities will help you get free from them so you can live a more authentic life. Today, I'm still a helpful person, but being able to consciously choose whether to help or not leaves me feeling happy in either situation.

What are some of your compensatory qualities? Write them in your journal.

You already know some of your positive qualities, and there are also many emergent qualities you'll grow throughout your life. Below is a list of positive qualities all human beings have at varying degrees. Be BOLD in claiming your positive qualities. Circle as many qualities as you know you have. I've bolded *courageous*, *resilient*, and *strong* for you because I know all survivors of childhood sexual abuse have these qualities.

After you've circled your positive qualities, write them in your journal. Don't worry if you can't name very many positive qualities, you can come back and add to this section later.

Accepting	Capable	Creative
Adventurous	Carefree	Curious
Approachable	Caring	Dedicated
Articulate	Charismatic	Dependable
Artistic	Cheerful	Determined
Assertive	Clever	Devoted
Authentic	Compassionate	Disciplined
Balanced	Confident	Discerning
Brave	Considerate	Empowering
Calm	**Courageous**	Energetic

Enthusiastic	Integral	Peaceful
Ethical	Joyful	Persevering
Fair	Kind	Playful
Flexible	Knowledgeable	Polite
Focused	Lively	Positive
Friendly	Love of Learning	Present
Fun	Loving	Reliable
Gentle	Loyal	**Resilient**
Genuine	Mature	Respectful
Giving	Mellow	Responsible
Graceful	Mindful	Self-motivated
Gracious	Modest	Sensitive
Grateful	Moral	Sincere
Hard-working	Motivated	Smart
Healthy	Natural	**Strong**
Helpful	Nonjudgmental	Sympathetic
Honest	Nurturing	Thoughtful
Humble	Open	Tolerant
Humorous	Open-minded	Transparent
Imaginative	Optimistic	Trustworthy
Independent	Organized	Upbeat
Influential	Outgoing	Wise
Innovative	Passionate	Witty
Insightful	Patient	

If you're still having difficulty naming your positive qualities, clues can be found in what your closest, most trusted friends have to say. Ask several people who know you well what qualities they most appreciate about you and write them down here and in your journal.

1.
2.
3.
4.
5.

Review the list again and choose three qualities you most want to grow.

Here are mine:

1. Adventurous
2. Influential
3. Passionate

What are the qualities you most want to grow?

1.
2.
3.

You don't need to know how to grow these qualities. Just naming them is enough for them to start developing. Take a few minutes to review your vision board and notice if the essence of these qualities is present in the images you chose. If not, then add a few images that do represent the qualities you most want to grow.

False Beliefs

Parents, deliberately or unaware, teach their children from birth how to behave, think, feel and perceive. Liberation from this influence is no easy matter.
~Eric Berne

You can turn lights on with a flick of a switch even if you don't understand how electricity works. However, if you understand how electricity works, then you can install a system that lights up your entire home.

If you understand the mechanics of any system, then you have more options to engage with that system.

It's the same with false beliefs. If you don't understand how false beliefs work, then they'll control how you think about yourself. In contrast, if you understand how false beliefs work, you can change how you feel about yourself and what you believe is possible for your life.

False Belief Definition: A misconception resulting from incorrect reasoning.

False beliefs are beliefs you make up about yourself, others, and life when you were too young to correctly interpret what happened. Children under the age of ten don't have the cognitive development for complex thinking. The younger you are, the more incapable you are of holding two conflicting ideas at the same time.

False beliefs are the result of internalizing abuse and believing what someone did to you is your fault. Some of the false beliefs I created include:

- I don't matter.
- I'm not loved.
- There's something wrong with me.

Core false beliefs feed themselves in a vicious repetitive cycle of self-forgetting.

People abandon themselves because of what they make up about themselves when the abuse happened. The interpretation of what happened gets turned into a core false belief which, over time, persistently shows up in a variety of life situations and you end up recreating the belief in current time.

For example, people who have a core belief they don't belong unconsciously set themselves up to not be included. Someone who doesn't believe they belong tends to isolate themselves and when they do participate will often show up late and leave early for events.

The false belief "I'm bad" is created from an intuitive sense that what someone is doing to them is bad. The young mind misinterprets "This is a bad thing happening to me" or "This person is doing a bad thing to me" to "I'm bad because this person did this to me."

The false belief "I don't matter" is created from knowing the person abusing them is treating them like they don't matter. If a person is abused, it doesn't mean they don't matter even though they might not matter to the person abusing them.

"There's something wrong happening" gets misinterpreted as "There's something wrong with me," and "This person isn't being loving to me" gets misinterpreted as "I'm unlovable."

False beliefs feel very personal and can be confusing and difficult to sort through to find what's true. It's confusing when the person who harms you also loves you, leaving you with a mistaken understanding of love in adulthood. If you live your life through the lens of a false belief, you might unconsciously believe you're only loved when someone is hurting you and unintentionally seek out people who end up harming you.

As you can see from the above examples, core false beliefs are some of the most important factors in determining the quality of your adult relationships. If you believe you have no value, then you'll unknowingly choose people to be in your life who treat you like you have no value. If you believe you don't matter, then you'll treat other people like they matter more than you *and* you'll let them treat you like you don't matter.

When the false belief "I don't matter" was prominent in my life, I ignored bad behavior from others who treated me like I don't matter. Only after I became aware of *treating myself like I didn't matter* was I able to address other people's bad behavior because that's what you do when you know you matter to yourself.

False Beliefs: How They Deepen over Time

The impact of seeing your world through a false belief is far reaching. The first time a child believes a false belief, it's like drawing a line on the ground. The child then retraces the line over new events they experience until the line becomes a deep groove that's difficult to climb out of. Imagine at the bottom of the groove is a rubber band holding the false belief tightly in place. The child tells their story over and over, often in the silence of their own mind, and by the time they become an adult the false belief is enmeshed in their psyche as if it were true.

The best indication of whether a false belief is running your life is by the experiences you're having and the choices you make. Here are a few ways you can know you're inside a false belief:

- You have difficulty setting clear boundaries because you're afraid of rejection.
- You stay in abusive relationships because you believe nobody will treat you better.
- You keep the meaning you make about circumstances to yourself instead of checking out their accuracy with other people.

False Beliefs: Gaining Freedom

False beliefs are your archenemy, and you must do everything in your power to break free of them. If you've unintentionally created a life from a false belief, then it will take conscious intention and effort to gain freedom from that false belief or beliefs. I felt like I was fighting for my life when I started questioning my false beliefs and began turning toward what's true.

Dismantling the false belief is like stretching the rubber band out of a groove. In the beginning, you may only get glimpses of what's true. The false belief holds tight and the elastic band snaps back the moment your attention wanders. Keep pulling on the elastic band by telling yourself what's true, and you'll create a new groove where you start living from the truth of who you are instead of the false beliefs that aren't good for you.

Gap Work: False Beliefs

Our minds have been poisoned and our accepted beliefs are unnatural and artificial.
~Bryant McGill

Get out your journal. Start gaining your freedom today by naming the false beliefs you created when you were very young. What's the most persistent thing you tell yourself when there's a crisis, a loss, or a hurt?

Here are common false beliefs survivors of childhood sexual abuse:

- I don't belong.
- I'm alone.
- I'm unsafe.
- I'm bad.
- I'm unworthy.

Whatever your core false belief is, write it below and in your journal.

My core false belief:

Now that you know what your core false belief is, answer these questions in your journal:

- In what ways do I hurt myself with this core false belief?
    Hurting yourself could include blaming other people for the quality of your relationships.

- In what ways do I compensate for this core false belief?
    Compensating could include overachieving or over-giving.

- In what ways do I energize this core false belief?
    Energizing false beliefs include ruminating over how the belief is true.

Now that you've named your core false belief and the impact, you can take the next step toward freedom.

Part Four
Repairing Your Relationship with Yourself

We repeat what we don't repair.
~Christine Langley-Obaugh

The work I did in therapy, both on my own and with my father, created new possibilities for me and my family. While my relationship with my father became healthy and strong as he took responsibility and made amends, the repair to our relationship didn't erase the impact of the abuse on my adult life and my most important intimate relationships.

Regardless of the responsibility someone takes for what they've done to you, regardless of any forgiveness you've extended, and regardless of any healing you now enjoy, abuse will have an impact on your adult life. The severity of that impact, however, is entirely up to you. You can lessen the impact of abuse on your life by repairing your relationship with yourself.

I was completely unaware of how false beliefs were impacting my life and how I felt about myself. I felt victimized by the sexual abuse and powerless to change what wasn't working for me. I believed the sexual abuse was the cause of all my pain and that *if only the abuse hadn't happened* then I wouldn't have any of the problems I was suffering with.

The bad news: You can't change anything that happened in the past. The abuse happened and it's over. Done!

Everything after sexual abuse was like living life through a hole-in-the-bucket, "I don't matter" lens. I couldn't see that the experiences I was having were connected to how I was treating myself and how I was letting others treat me. As I made choices in line with someone who believed they didn't matter, I deepened the conviction that I didn't matter.

Once you become aware of how you're making choices through the meaning you gave to what happened, you'll be able to access the power to stop unconsciously recreating your felt childhood experience in current time.

The problem isn't what happened to you; the problem is the world you create after what happened to you.

The good news is that you have complete power to lessen the impact abuse has on your present life by changing how you relate to the past. It's not the past you need to repair; it's your relationship with yourself in current time that you need to repair.

When you take responsibility by consciously choosing the meaning you make about what happened, new choices will become available to you. As you make choices you haven't made before, you'll get results you haven't gotten before, guaranteed.

The Inner Child

She held herself until the sobs of the child inside subsided entirely. I love you, she told herself. It will all be okay.
~H Raven Rose, Shadow Selves

It's easier to get free of the past when you understand how the psyche works in relationship to the concept of the inner child. This concept was first introduced by psychologist Carl Jung. Jung believed the inner child deeply influenced everything we do and all the decisions we make as adults.

We act or react from our early wounding, interpreting life and interactions through the lens of what we believe about ourselves. You've seen it—people behaving like little children instead of healthy responsible adults. You've personally experienced it yourself—as have I.

It's common to feel the same way you felt as when the abuse first happened. The past gets collapsed onto your present life and the child part of you takes over. I call this an enmeshment between the child and who you are today. You can recognize when this is happening when you engage in childlike behaviors or express feelings in childlike ways. When your past is collapsed onto you in present time, it feels like you're right back in your childhood—but you're not. There's only the adult you are today and *the memory of what happened* to you as a child.

Regardless of having been hurt in the past, you can grow up and embody the adult you are today. It takes a high level of self-awareness to start integrating your difficult past experiences, but you can do it. You can learn how to include your early wounding while not acting out early wounding in your most important relationships, or in any area of your daily life.

Repairing your relationship with yourself requires truth telling, but telling the truth to yourself when you're enmeshed with the wounded child only leaves you feeling shame—it will keep you stuck. To repair your relationship with yourself, you must tell yourself the truth while being anchored in your adult self. When the hurt part feels safe, your younger self can take refuge in *your* adult arms. Then you can give yourself what you most need to receive.

Since you can only change what you're aware of, you'll need to invest time and energy learning how the inner child impacts your life today so you can tell yourself the truth. You can raise your awareness and begin to repair your relationship by listening to the hurt part of you.

Listening to the Hurt Part

Your inner child is waiting for a genuine, heartfelt apology.
~Yong Kang Chan, Parent Yourself Again: Love Yourself the Way You Have Always Wanted to Be Loved

If I could give you only one exercise to repair your relationship between you and the younger wounded part of yourself, it would be the Inner Sanctuary of Safety with Tonglen created by my good friend Katherine Woodward Thomas, *New York Times* bestselling author of *Conscious Uncoupling: 5 Steps to Living Happily Even After* and *Calling in "The One": 7 Weeks to Attract the Love of Your Life.*

In the Inner Sanctuary of Safety with Tonglen you'll name your feelings and needs, which were rarely validated for most children. It's more likely that you were talked, or bullied, out of your feelings and needs. In the best of situations, caregivers dismiss, minimize, or redirect children's difficult feelings, and it can sound something like this:

- Go to your room and don't come out until you can put on a happy face.
- Stop crying or I'll give you something to cry about.
- (Eyeroll) Here we go again.
- You shouldn't feel that way.
- Crybaby.

It's worse when sexual abuse is present.

Because of the secrecy that often comes with childhood sexual abuse, children tend to suffer in silence, getting more disconnected from their feelings and needs. A child's survival depends on their caregivers, no matter how inadequate or abusive the circumstances, so give yourself compassion instead of judgment if you abandoned yourself.

There was a good reason to abandon yourself and disconnect from your feelings and needs at the time of the abuse—as a kid, shutting down was a brilliant way to survive the experience. But today, shutting down creates suffering. Today, you need to be connected to your feelings and needs to thrive in your life.

The Inner Sanctuary of Safety with Tonglen will help you reconnect with your feelings and needs so you can create deep authentic connection with yourself and others. I'll explain how to use the Inner Sanctuary of Safety with Tonglen so you can get the most value out of the exercise, including crucial distinctions to guide your experience. The entire exercise is at the end of this section so you can follow along step-by-step.

Inner Sanctuary of Safety with Tonglen Distinctions

An important distinction to keep in mind as you engage in this exercise is the difference between inner child work and the repair done using the Inner Sanctuary of Safety with Tonglen.

With inner child work, you might process the pain you feel by acting out the feelings you're having, or you might cry or have a tantrum.

Using the Inner Sanctuary of Safety with Tonglen as a relationship repair, you don't process your feelings. Instead, you become the healthy adult who powerfully holds the difficult feelings and needs of the hurt part of you.

There are several things to keep in mind as you do the Inner Sanctuary of Safety:

- Stay connected to your adult self in present time.

The main misunderstanding I've seen people make using this exercise is to confuse the adult part with the child part. Remember that this isn't an inner-child exercise, this is a repair exercise between you and you—between your adult self and your child self. Throughout the entire exercise, stay grounded in the adult part of you while turning your attention toward the young part of you who was hurt.

- The child didn't do anything wrong, so the child can't be responsible for the repair. Only the adult part of you can repair your relationship with the hurt part of you.

Children have yet to develop the capacities to understand the complexity of the feelings they have. They often believe they're at fault and go into shame about what happened to them and what they're feeling. Children also dissociate to protect themselves from difficult or confusing emotions. It's understandable if you have a difficult time with big emotions.

If you didn't have someone to guide you as a child, then you probably don't know how to relate to your emotions in healthy ways as an adult. No worries, you can start learning now.

- Stop the exercise if you collapse into your emotions and try again later.

Since this isn't an inner-child exercise, don't fall apart. If a young child who was hurt the way you were hurt came to you for help, would you collapse into tears and let them take care of you? No, it wouldn't be appropriate. You would do whatever it takes to stay strong and alert for the little one, so immerse yourself in adult consciousness and don't fall into the child consciousness.

The most apparent indication you're losing connection with the adult part of you is if you start to collapse into a wounded feeling state. You might start to cry, feel helpless, or shrink your body. If you continue to collapse, you might even dissociate and leave your body. If you notice this starting to happen, simply stop the exercise and bring yourself into the present moment. Reconnect with the adult part of you and begin again. If you have difficulty connecting with the adult part of you, then you can try again later.

Here are several ways to stop an emotional collapse from happening:

- Open your eyes and tell yourself out loud what city you're in and what day it is.
- Open your eyes and look around the room. Notice the color of the walls and if there are windows or doors.
- Open your eyes and feel your body. Feel your feet on the floor. Move your toes. Stand up and bounce on the balls of your feet.
- Open your eyes and take a conscious slow breath and notice the rise and fall of your belly.
- Open your eyes and stand up. Put your shoulders back and slightly lift your chin.

When you're ready to begin again, imagine the energy in your body entering the earth like a stake in the ground—strong and stable. Open your arms and your heart to hold the tender child in your lap and begin again.

Gap Work: Inner Sanctuary of Safety

Care for your psyche… know thyself, for once we know ourselves, we may learn how to care for ourselves.
~ Socrates

Inner Sanctuary of Safety with Tonglen Created by Katherine Woodward Thomas[3]

1. **Become Still.** Find a quiet space to sit for a few minutes. If it is safe to do so, close your eyes and take a deep breath, as though you could breathe all the way down into your hips. Moving into a place of deep listening and receptivity, become aware of the feelings and sensations in your body and release any tension you might be holding.

2. **Step Back from Your Feelings.** Imagine being able to step back from your many thoughts and feelings and notice there's a part of you able to simply witness yourself having these thoughts and feelings with a deep sense of care, compassion, and curiosity. Notice the witness within has access to wisdom and maturity and you're able to see what's happening in your life from a larger and more well-informed perspective.

3. **Connect with a Deeper, Wider Center Within.** Keep breathing. As you do, become aware there is a center within you that is deeper and wider than the feelings you're having, where you can know and experience, if only for a brief moment, how you're okay in spite of all you are going through.

4. **Extend Love to the Part of You Suffering.** From this deeper, mature, and wiser center within, extend love to the part of you which is feeling overwhelmed with negative emotions. Give this hurting part of you your full attention while staying identified with your mature and wise witness self. Notice where in your body you are holding these difficult emotions and offer this suffering part of you support and compassion.

---

[3] Woodward Thomas, Katherine. *Conscious Uncoupling: 5 Steps to Living Happily Even After* (2015). Used by permission of Harmony Books, an imprint of Random House, a division of Penguin Random House LLC. All rights reserved.

5. **Welcome In and Mirror Your Feelings.** With deep kindness and compassion, ask yourself the following question:

   "What are you feeling, sweetheart?"

   Listen closely for the response and then lovingly mirror it back by saying to yourself:

   "I can see you're feeling _____ [sad, enraged, hopeless, used, etc.]."

   NOTE: Try broadening your emotional vocabulary by stretching to name the specific feeling you're having. For example, rather than just saying "depressed," look to find a word that more accurately names your experience, such as *despondent, desperate,* or *hopeless.*

   Continue asking the question "What are you feeling, sweetheart?" until all your feelings have been named and mirrored.

1. **Breathe out a Blessing.** For each feeling you identify, on your next in breath, breathe the feeling straight into the center of your heart, fully welcoming it, and on the out breath, breathe out a prayer and blessing for yourself and all beings throughout the world who are suffering with this exact same feeling in this very moment. Repeat until all the feelings you are currently experiencing have been tended to.

2. **Name and Mirror Your Needs.** Now, with deep kindness and compassion, ask yourself the following question: "What do you need, sweetheart?"

   Listen closely for the response and then lovingly mirror it back by saying to yourself: "I can see you need _____ [love, closure, an apology, justice, safety, support, comfort, to be seen, to be heard, etc.]."

   NOTE: While it may be tempting to jump into action to try to fulfill your needs, please recognize the simple act of attending to yourself is what is most important. Not every need can be met immediately, but all can be counted as valid or worthy of your attention. This is particularly vital if the person you loved was incapable or unwilling to tend to your needs or take them seriously.

Continue to ask the question "What do you need, sweetheart?" until all your needs have been named and mirrored.

To get the full benefit of the Inner Sanctuary of Safety with Tonglen and experience profound results, I recommend doing this exercise at least three times per day for two weeks.

Therapists and coaches alike report getting the same amazing results with their clients as I do with mine. If you commit yourself to the Inner Sanctuary of Safety with Tonglen as I have recommended, then I'm confident you'll also get huge results. You'll experience increased compassion toward the hurt part of you which has been trying to get your attention.

Banishing the hurt part of you won't work, but communicating with the hurt part of you through the Inner Sanctuary of Safety with Tonglen can. Learning how to name your feelings and needs is a necessary skill you can learn. Instead of reacting to what you're unconsciously feeling or needing, you can develop your capacity to notice, name, and allow your feelings to be where they are without judgment.

Being aware of your feelings and needs inside of an adult center will give you power over reactionary patterns from the past. You can learn to consciously choose whether to take action based on what's needed for each circumstance or situation you're in.

NOTE: Some people benefit from being guided through this exercise. If you feel this would serve you, then use the QR code below to go to my website and schedule a session with me.

Forgiveness

Holding on to pain, anger, guilt, or shame is the glue that binds us to the situation we want to escape.
~Iyanla Vanzant

Forgiveness doesn't mean forgetting what happened or erasing wrongdoing. Forgiveness never means sexual abuse is okay. More accurately, forgiveness is the doorway to stop living through the hurts of the past. Forgiveness lifts a weight off your shoulders so you can move forward in your life.

It was easier to blame my father for not having the life I wanted than to go out and create it for myself. Focusing on what he did instead of what I could do kept me stuck. What my father did impacts my life, but it no longer defines me in negative ways. Once I forgave myself for letting the past have power over me, I was able to do the hard work in creating the life I'm now living.

Here's a forgiveness prayer I start my day with. I hope it brings you the peace I've found.

Comprehensive Forgiveness Prayer for Ourselves[4]

Offered by John Newton

You may speak this prayer aloud or silently as many times daily as you feel. Positive effects have been reported in many areas of life from this simple practice. Ten or more times will bring optimal results, but even one or two times each day will not only anchor the results you received in the live, virtual, or recorded session but also address future karma. As the prayers are encoded with a direct connection to consciousness and the intelligence structured within it, reading/

---

[4] Used with permission from the author, John Newton. Health Beyond Belief website.

speaking them connects you with the true source of all health and well-being: The Creator.

Infinite Creator, All You Are: For me, all my family members, all our relationships, all our ancestors and all their relationships through all time, through all our lives.

For all hurts and wrongs: Physical, mental, emotional, spiritual, sexual, and financial through thought, word, or deed: Please help us all forgive each other, forgive ourselves, forgive all people and all people forgive us, completely and totally. Please and thank you.

For all suicide, incest, murder, rape, abortion, and infidelity through thought, word, or deed: Please help us all forgive each other, forgive ourselves, forgive all people and all people forgive us, completely and totally. Please and thank you.

For all times we abandoned or were abandoned; withheld love or had love withheld; weren't nurtured, loved, and supported and times we didn't nurture, love, or support others: Infinite Creator, please help us all forgive, be forgiven and all forgive ourselves, completely and totally. Please and thank you.

Please Infinite Creator, for the highest good: Lift out all weight, pain, burden, sin, death, debt, negativity, and limitation of all kinds; transform it into your love, and let your love flow back into us, filling and giving us all complete peace, now and forever. Please and thank you. Please and thank you. Please and thank you.

Please help us love and bless each other; love and bless ourselves. Be at peace with each other and at peace with ourselves, now and forever. Please and thank you.

Once you make the distinction between the sexual abuse (what happened *to* you) and how you relate to the sexual abuse (what you tell yourself *about* the sexual abuse), you'll likely feel the need to forgive yourself.

Remember, any abuse inflicted on you could never be your fault so there's no need to forgive yourself for what someone else did to you. However, you do need to forgive yourself if you *believe* what happened to you was your fault. You also need to forgive yourself for the ways you've been recreating the abuse in your adult life.

Below is an ancient Hawaiian prayer you can also use for self-forgiveness.

Gap Work: Ho'oponopono

The weak can never forgive. Forgiveness is the attribute of the strong.
~Mahatma Gandhi, All Men are Brothers: Autobiographical Reflections

In the Ho'oponopono[5] practice, you're asking for self-forgiveness for the harm you've done to yourself by believing any abuse was your fault.

Get out your journal. Set aside fifteen minutes for this exercise. For the first ten minutes write about what you most need to forgive yourself for. Ask yourself the following:

- What choices have I made that I know aren't good for me?
- Specifically, what do I do or say to myself that I would not do or say to anyone else?
- What beliefs about myself have been the most harmful?
- How have I let the abuse define and confine me?
- In what ways have I not lived up to my potential?

Follow these steps to practice the Ho'oponopono prayer:

1. Find a peaceful quiet space to sit for about five minutes.
2. Close your eyes and take a few slow deep breaths.
3. Bring into your awareness one of the ways you need to forgive yourself.
4. Slowly repeat the mantra seven to ten times: "I'm sorry. Please forgive me. Thank you. I love you."

These simple phrases organically help you to be more loving toward yourself.

1. Sit in silence after you end your last repetition and take a few slow breaths into your belly.
2. Repeat for each area you want to forgive yourself for.

---

[5] *Ho'oponopono* is an ancient Hawaiian spiritual practice that is based on the principles of repentance, gratitude, and responsibility for the world. Its origins are deeply rooted in profound spiritual teachings, which would originally be facilitated by a revered elder of the community. It has been brought into modern day spiritual practice as a short four-line prayer that can be used by any individual as a personal healing prayer of forgiveness for self and others.

You can use this self-forgiveness prayer as often as you want and notice how self-compassion starts to grow within you.

Making Sacred Commitments

> *Freedom is not the absence of commitments, but the ability to choose—and commit myself to—what is best for me.*
> *~Paulo Coelho*

Repairing your relationship with yourself requires that you make and keep commitments with yourself. Relating to these commitments as sacred can help you take them seriously and remember that you're inherently worthy of having a life free from the pain and shame of childhood sexual abuse.

I recommend starting with making these two sacred commitments to yourself:

1. Treat yourself with compassion.
2. Establish self-care practices.

These sacred commitments can feel a little awkward in the beginning. With consistent and persistent attention, the practice will get easier and, over time, treating yourself with compassion and taking good care of yourself will become your new comfort zone.

Sacred Commitment #1: Treat Yourself with Compassion

> *You've been criticizing yourself for years and it hasn't worked. Try approving of yourself and see what happens.*
> *~Louise L. Hay*

Compassion is what you feel when you know someone is suffering and feel motivated to ease their pain. Compassion includes kindness and empathy toward someone who has lived through abuse, and being patient and warm toward someone who is hurting. People who have been abused as children often treat others with a high level of compassion while being overly harsh toward themselves. Withholding compassion from yourself is a subtle unconscious way of victimizing yourself and reinforcing feelings of unworthiness.

Brain scans, such as those done by the National Institute for Health, show the area of the brain impacted by abuse. Research shows that self-compassion helps you feel better after difficult situations including the trauma experienced from abuse.[6] The significance of the scientific research shows that you have the power to ease your own pain by extending compassion toward yourself. Getting free of the pain and shame of childhood sexual abuse requires taking responsibility for learning how to show yourself compassion, which organically leads to a better relationship with yourself. Compassion includes acknowledging the pain, sincerely listening, and being supportive and encouraging.

Giving myself compassion helped me see that having needs is part of being human. As I extended compassion to myself, I became kinder and gentler toward myself. The more compassion I gave to myself, the easier it became to make the changes I needed to make. In the beginning, treating myself with compassion felt awkward, but over time, a new habit developed and now compassion for myself comes naturally. Today, self-compassion makes it possible for me to share my story and honor what I've lived through without falling into despair.

Let's identify where you most need to treat yourself with compassion and then take a step toward giving yourself compassion.

Gap Work: Where Do You Need Self-Compassion?

> *Feeling compassion for ourselves in no way releases us from responsibility for our actions. Rather, it releases us from the self-hatred that prevents us from responding to our life with clarity and balance.*
> ~Tara Brach

There's nobody who can understand what you went through and the impact to your life better than you can. You lived it.

---

[6] https://www.ncbi.nlm.nih.gov/pmc/articles/PMC3181836/

Extending compassion to myself was elusive for many years. I judged myself for having needs. I made it wrong that I had needs and hid them as best I could. While pushing my needs away, I covertly, unconsciously, and passive-aggressively grasped for others to meet my needs.

What most calls for your compassion are the places where you're hardest on yourself and where you most judge yourself as being bad or wrong, the parts you don't like about yourself, and the parts you feel ashamed of and want to hide from yourself and the world.

Get out your journal and answer these questions:

- What do I most judge about myself?
- What do I most make wrong about myself?
- What's the consistent habitual internal dialogue I say to myself?

After considering everything you wrote, what do you most need to give yourself compassion for? Write this in your journal.

> *Self-compassion is simply giving the same kindness to ourselves that we would give to others.*
> *~Christopher Germer*

One way I've been able to extend compassion to myself is to imagine myself at the age I was harmed. If it's too difficult to imagine yourself at this age, then imagine another child the same age as you were. Try it now.

Standing firmly in your adult self, bring forth a vision of your younger self or a child the same age you were when you were hurt. If you can, use a photograph of yourself under the age of ten to connect with this younger self.

If you're using the image of another young child, then imagine they had the same experiences you did and was hurt in the same way you were hurt. Imagine they believed the same things you believed about yourself at that time.

Look into the child's eyes and tell them what you would say to any child who had the same experience as you had. Do it now. Tell them you love them, and that they didn't do anything wrong.

Take a few minutes to tell them anything else you want them to know. Tell them what you most wanted someone to say to you.

Once you've said everything you want them to know, imagine this young innocent person getting smaller and smaller until you can fit them into the palm of your hand. Then breathe them into your heart where they can live and feel safe and loved. Tell them you've got them and they're right where they belong, in the center of your heart.

*Bonus Practice: Once you've completed this visualization, use a photo of yourself under the age of ten, or at the age you were harmed. Place the photo where you can easily see it and take about five minutes every day to look into the innocent eyes of your younger self and extend compassion to this precious being. If it brings up emotions, let them flow.

Yoga and Compassion

A study by the Department of Social Work shows that trauma experts are seeing evidence that doing yoga builds a survivor's capacity for self-compassion, which has been shown to be an effective healing method for survivors of sexual abuse.

One of the simplest yoga practices is pranayama or breathing practice. If you're able to, sit in a comfortable position. Begin by taking a few natural breaths. Follow your breath in through your nose and draw it to the back of your throat and deep into your belly. Feel the warmth of your breath as it leaves your body keeping your attention in your belly.

Take a few more slow, deep breaths moving your attention from the top of your head through the center of your body and into the belly, then from your belly through the center of your body out the bottom of your feet. With your next breath, draw it from the bottom of your feet through the center of your body into your belly and exhale at the top of your head. Repeat for several breaths.

Notice thoughts as they arise with your inhale and let them go with your exhale.

Continue this practice several times throughout the day and notice a softening and compassionate holding of yourself.

Take about five minutes to write in your journal about what you notice.

Sacred Commitment #2: Establish Self-Care Practices

> *If you feel lost, disappointed, hesitant, or weak, return to yourself, to who you are, here and now and when you get there, you will discover yourself, like a lotus flower in full bloom, even in a muddy pond, beautiful and strong.*
> ~Masaru Emoto

Tendencies toward a lack of self-care start very young. Children make inaccurate interpretations based on their age and current level of development. My self-abandonment began with the interpretation I made at the time of the abuse: "I don't matter." If I don't matter, then a child's thinking logic also says my needs don't matter. My need for safety, love, attention, care, and consideration didn't matter. I didn't understand the words, "My needs don't matter." Instead, I lived my life through a feeling in my body that none of my needs mattered. It was near impossible to prioritize self-care while believing I didn't matter, but prioritizing self-care is like medicine when you're healing the impact of past abuse.

Establishing self-care practices is essential for healing to take root, yet true self-care can be elusive. Many abuse survivors feel they must sacrifice their own care for others and feel guilty when they first start committing to self-care practices.

It isn't easy to engage in self-care while living in a culture that rewards self-abandonment and judges self-care as selfish. Self-care can be healthy or unhealthy. Taking care of yourself in unhealthy ways can be seen in unconscious behaviors such as:

- Being overly dependent to get others to take care of you.
- Being overly focused on your own needs at the expense of everyone else.

Your commitment to self-care supports your commitment to healing. Let's take a step toward healthy self-care.

Gap Work: Prioritizing Self-Care

*Self-care is giving the world what's best for you,
instead of what's left of you.*
~Katie Reed

Get your journal. Before we identify healthy self-care practices, we need to look at ways you *avoid* taking care of yourself.

Set aside about fifteen minutes for this exercise. Keep your list nearby so you can add to it later.

Step 1—Identify how you're cared for by others.

- Describe your experience of being cared for when you were a child.
- In what ways do you not feel cared for today?
- How do the people closest to you tend to treat you?
- How does the way you're being cared for today feel like how you were cared for in your early years?

It's normal to experience difficult feelings as you raise your consciousness regarding the care which was missing from early caregivers or others you've been in close relationship with as an adult. Thinking about all the ways you weren't cared for may bring awareness of sadness, anger, disappointment, or even resentment around all the ways you haven't been cared for in the past.

Now let's look at how you've been treating yourself, so you can take another step toward freedom.

Step 2—Identify all the ways you avoid taking care of yourself.

- In what ways do you abandon yourself? Notice if these ways are consistent and habitual.
- Notice any place you habitually keep your commitment to others but not to yourself.
- In what ways do you focus on taking care of others at your own expense?
- Make a list of all the things you would like to give yourself but haven't. Include the ways you habitually avoid prioritizing your need for sleep, nourishment, nutrition, fun and play, or anything else you know is good for you.

If you've been self-abandoning, don't assume immediate change. Learning to prioritize self-care can feel like a scary roller-coaster ride, but it's okay to prioritize yourself. When you're sufficiently caring for yourself at the deepest level, you'll also begin to care for others in more authentic and balanced healthy ways.

Step 3—Identify self-care practices.

Self-care practices should include specific loving self-care behaviors. Perhaps caring for yourself is having a bubble bath or getting your nails done. One way I like to care for myself is having someone wash and blow-dry my hair. Self-care always includes getting enough sleep and exercise. Self-care also includes choosing people to be in your life who hold you in love. Identify what feels like self-care to you by answering the following questions:

- How do you secretly wish to be taken care of?
- What are some of the ways you want to be nurtured?
- What kind of care do you long for?

Step 4—Make a commitment.

Now take responsibility for giving yourself the care you need. Following through on the choices you make around how you want to care for yourself is super important and will naturally lead others to do the same.

Make a list of self-care behaviors you're willing to commit to. Check the ones you are willing to try or add your own.

- Drink half your body weight in ounces of water every day.
- Get at least eight to ten hours of sleep every night. Research shows going to bed by 10 p.m. offers the most health protection.
- Exercise for thirty minutes at least three times per week.
- Sit for a regular and consistent prayer or meditation practice.
- Spend time in nature every day.
- Put your bare feet on the ground at least once per day. Feel the earth underneath you, supporting your weight, and breathe.
- Take time for yourself each week to do something you love.
- Read a book you've been putting off.
- Have breakfast in bed.
- Take a nourishing bath.
- Take a slow walking meditation.
- Sun gaze with eyes closed for two minutes per day.
- Hug a tree.
- Hike or climb a mountain.
- Go camping.

Here are some ways to support self-care practices:

- Live in the present moment.

Deep self-care may include doing nothing at all. Maybe you sit with yourself and take a slow walk at the end of your day. Presence will replace dissociation and you'll experience self-care simply by being in your body. Self-care can be as natural as letting energy move through you without having to do anything.

- Conscious breathing.

I've discovered that avoidance deepens pain instead of making it go away. Slow conscious breathing allows pain to move through the body and pass like a wave. You may feel more pain in the beginning but just sit with the sensations and breathe. It could take thirty seconds or five minutes to move through but stay with your breath and notice the pain does move.

Here are some suggestions on how to allow the pain to pass through:

- If thoughts arise, let them pass instead of focusing on them. Don't add meaning or a story about what you're feeling. Just breathe. Don't name the feeling or the circumstance. Just breathe.
- Keep your attention on the movement of your breath starting with breathing in through your nose and drawing your breath deep into your belly. Follow the breath with your awareness as it slowly enters and leaves your body.

With practice, you'll learn how to let your feelings move through you and self-care will become easier.

Your commitment to self-care supports your commitment to heal. Give yourself time for an organic shift to take place, and it will. Eventually you'll find the sweet spot where you make your self-care a priority, but not at the expense of anything or anyone that matters to you. When you're present to what is needed and what life is asking of you, you'll be able to choose in the moment the most caring choice.

Part Five
Victimization vs. Responsibility

In violence, we forget who we are.
~Mary McCarthy.

It is through violence that our souls come... into focus.
~Maggie Nelson, The Art of Cruelty: A Reckoning

The above quotes illustrate how abuse cuts us off from ourselves while at the same time opening the possibility to discover the deeper truth of who we really are. The very human, healing journey is about reconnecting with innate sacredness. No matter what awful things happen, you can write a more accurate story—one that illuminates your courage and perseverance.

For me, sexual abuse was like being sucked into a black hole where I lost connection with myself. What I was able to create in my life was filtered through a self-constructed belief I was insignificant. The belief I didn't matter informed every part of my life. I treated myself as the least important person in my life. Believing the story I told myself made it easy to drink heavily, to be promiscuous, to marry an alcoholic, and to damage the most important relationships in my life. These are all ways I treated myself like I didn't matter.

Here's an important distinction which leads to freedom:

You create your experience through your beliefs, and through the meaning you make out of what happens to you.

Until this distinction is understood and you become aware of how you've been living life through the meanings you make, you'll continue to create a world which is limiting to you.

Differentiating between what is and isn't your responsibility is a necessary skill. Taking responsibility isn't about blaming yourself for what happened to you when you were a child. Taking responsibility isn't about letting others off the hook for hurting you. You're *never* responsible for the abuse inflicted on you. *Ever!*

In contrast to not being responsible for the abuse, you *are* responsible for the life you create once you're an adult. **You regain your power by raising your awareness and by taking responsibility for all aspects of your life after the abuse ends and you're an adult.**

- You're *always* responsible for the meaning you make about the abuse.
- You're *always* responsible for the choices you make once you're an adult.
- You're *always* responsible for getting the help you need to free yourself.

Taking 100 percent responsibility is a choice to step into your personal power and to no longer be dominated by what happened to you in the past.

It's difficult to create a happy life without understanding how the meanings we make contribute to the pain we feel today. If the abuse isn't happening now, but you feel very much the same way about yourself and your life as when the abuse happened, then you're living your life through the beliefs you made up when the abuse happened.

You're way more powerful than letting the past limit you. I know you are. To start getting free, you must learn how to stop blaming yourself, or the person who hurt you, for the life you have today. They're not hurting you now.

I unconsciously and silently took responsibility for the abuse inflicted on me. Instead of placing the responsibility for my father's behavior on him and making it mean his behavior was wrong, I made it mean I must have done something to provoke the abuse. I truly believed I would get in trouble for what my father did while at the same time blaming myself for not telling someone and getting the help I needed.

Because I believed I didn't matter, I learned many ways to treat myself like I didn't matter.

- I internalized the responsibility and made it mean I didn't matter.
- Taking responsibility for what was *not* mine led to my excessive drinking to get away from how bad I felt about myself.

- I ignored myself so I wouldn't feel the pain of not mattering again.
- I agreed with others without contributing my opinions to protect myself from possibly feeling rejected.
- I focused on other people's dreams instead of my own.
- I went along with things I didn't want to go along with.
- I didn't take the time to discover what really mattered to me.
- I chose codependent relationships.
- I lived far below my potential.

With the help of a therapist and coach, I realized *my behavior* after the abuse was a reaction to the abuse that happened long ago. I began to see that I was taking responsibility for harm I didn't cause and wasn't taking responsibility for doing what I needed to do to create the life I wanted.

Gaining freedom from a wounded past requires taking responsibility for the future you want to create. This future always includes learning how to relate to yourself and others in healthy ways. As you become healthier, you'll begin to tap into a more authentic version of yourself.

Always remember you're not responsible for what happened to you. Today, you're responsible for all the choices you make as an adult including how you interpret the abuse and the meaning you make about it. Anything else is to live inside of victimization. To stop living in reaction to the abuse and to step into a level of responsibility and generate the life you want, you'll need to break up with all forms of victimization.

Breaking Up with Victimization

*Life will give you whatever experience is most
helpful for the evolution of your consciousness.*
~Eckhart Tolle

Being on a healing journey generally includes having done a significant amount of personal work to deal with early victimization. Getting unstuck and gaining freedom from the past takes time and commitment to let go of the tendency to see oneself as a victim. Remnants of victimhood can feel like tendrils holding relational dynamics tightly in place that originated early in life. Feeling like we have no control over what keeps happening to us in adult life can be a subtle way we're embedded in the victimization of the past.

Habitual patterns continue to show up because we're used to them; they're familiar. Human beings seek out the familiar. When something is "known" we can count on it and handle whatever happens. The familiar, while not giving us the life we want, can feel like the safest way of living. No wonder we stay feeling like a victim. Changing habits is like stepping into an unknown, unsafe territory and can feel very scary.

Individuals who are stuck in victimization can be exceptionally hard on themselves. They can have a difficult time distancing themselves from the past and there can be an unconscious loyalty to victimization. Tendencies toward remaining a victim cross many cultural differences as does the universal longing for freedom from the past.

> I was a happy nine-year-old—without a care in the world. Every day was the same; I came home from school each day, confident there would be homework, yardwork, and something yummy my mother would be cooking on the stove.
>
> One day was different from the rest—a day that would confuse any young child. I arrived home from school and the stove wasn't even

warm. I called for my mother, but she didn't answer. I searched every room in the house but couldn't find her.

I called my father at work. The extent of the conversation between us included only one question and one answer.

"Where's Mom?" I asked.

"She's at home," my father answered.

Nope. She wasn't. But I looked for her again.

My mother had moved out without telling anyone.

My father was not prepared for my mother leaving suddenly. He ignored her disappearance and simply made dinner when he got home and took us to school the next morning with no explanation.

I continued to go to school for three months without knowing what happened to my mother. Then one day I came home to find my mother in the kitchen. There was hot food on the stove and the laundry had been done.

I felt as confused about her coming home as I was about her leaving. With no discussion from my parents, I went to school the next day and carried on as if she had never left.

My mother was home, and I was happy again—until it happened again. And again.

My mother's lengthy coming and going continued without any explanation. I loved coming home to a clean home, a meal on the table, and my mother drinking Dr. Pepper. Each time she returned, I pretended she hadn't left. Each time she left I deepened the belief I didn't matter to her. An adult can understand it wasn't the child's fault, but the child makes it mean that they don't matter. "If I mattered, why would she leave?" is the question I asked myself.

My mother's dysfunctional behavior continued, and I shut down to the pain of believing I didn't matter to my own mother by telling myself that she didn't matter to me. I started lashing out at her and told anyone who would listen how she hurt me and how I was the victim of her wrongdoing. My mother couldn't win in the face of my pain, and I told my story far into adulthood. I felt victimized by my mother's presence *and* her absence. I collected evidence that I didn't matter to her and interpreted everything she did and didn't do to mean she was hurting me on purpose. Oh, what pain I caused myself in blaming her and taking what she did personally.

Gaining freedom from the past is only possible when you can hold more than one truth at a time. The child part cannot hold two truths at the same time. The fact my mother hurt me was one truth. That she didn't love me the way I need to be loved is also true. Another truth is that her lack of capacity wasn't personal to me. My mother was also deeply wounded from her childhood. She loved me to the capacity she was able to, given her own life experiences and early wounding.

Being able to hold more than one perspective without minimizing either can only be done when you're connected with the adult part of yourself. Individuating from my mother and finding my adult part was almost as painful as being enmeshed with her. I participated in a workshop called Healing the Mother Wound facilitated by Shauna Wilson, a wise woman. One of the exercises during the event was to make a paper mâché mask of my face.

> I lay on the floor. Music was playing. I felt the coolness of the wet strips of plaster being layered onto my face by another workshop participant. The mask dried enough to take it off my face, and I placed it on the ground and went for a walk.
>
> When I returned to a completely dried mask, I was instructed to put the mask back on my face and imagine breathing my mother into me. I contemplated the impact my mother had on my life and all I felt was anger. I rejected her wholeheartedly.
>
> Everyone else's mask fit their own face like a glove, and mine did too, but I refused to believe this was MY mask. I had rejected my mother so much I couldn't let myself be anything like her.
>
> I felt victimized by the other women in the workshop and accused them of playing a trick on me. I was convinced they had traded my mask for another. I reacted like a rebellious teen and decorated my mask through seething anger and frustration.
>
> My mother loved her jewelry, and I hated her jewelry. More accurately, I was jealous of her jewelry. In my childhood interpretation, I believed that she loved her jewelry more than she loved me. So, I decorated my mask while being focused on what I least liked about my mother—I judged her for being materialistic and I used gobs of costume jewelry. It was easier to judge my mother and make her

wrong for being materialistic than to feel the heartbreak of how little I felt loved by her.

Since I didn't want to be like my mother, I NEVER wore jewelry. Fully expressing my contempt for her, I decorated my mask with jewelry coming out of her mouth. I distanced myself from my mother and the mask and complained about the exercise for the rest of the weekend.

After the weekend was over, I put the mask in the back of my car. I started backing up to leave and for the first time I saw my mother's face reflected in the rear-view mirror. Compassion for both me and my mother flooded my heart; I stopped the car and sobbed.

I spent decades judging my mother and making her wrong for simply being her wounded self. It was a long journey toward total forgiveness, but I was finally on the path of forgiving my mother for not being able to give me what I needed. I was also on the path of forgiving myself for holding her with unrealistic expectations and making her responsible for what I hadn't been able to create in my adult life.

I drove home and began another layer of forgiveness and healing, but my mother wasn't available to participate. She hadn't spoken to me for a couple of years when I received a phone call.

"We've been keeping this from you, and I think you deserve to know that your mother has stage 4 colon cancer and is going to die." Again, I stopped and sobbed.

This call was another opportunity to take responsibility for what was mine.

Thinking it was the last time I would see my mother, I packed a bag and drove two hours to the hospital where she would be having surgery the next day. When she realized it was me who came to visit, she kicked me out of her room and refused to see me.

I stayed in my car that night and wrote nonstop until the sun came up. I contemplated my life and relationship with her. I thought about how hurt I felt and how I still longed for her love.

Memories of my early life flooded me. My mother was only sixteen when she got married and couldn't possibly have known what she was doing. Again, I had compassion for how hard it must have been on my mother to be so young and inexperienced with life. On the tear-stained pages, I let it all go. All remaining hurt and anger drained from my heart, and I was free.

An open, broken heart helped me understand my mother did the best she could. Staying present to the adult part of me, I could see where I both needed something from my mother and could understand that her *not* having what I needed didn't mean she didn't love me. My mother simply didn't have the awareness she needed. She didn't take responsibility for learning how to create a healthy family.

I would not have needed anything from her if she had died that day. She didn't die that day and she made it clear that she didn't want anything to do with me. Over the next ten months, I contacted my mother on a regular basis and each time I got the same response. "Mom, I love..." click. Right in the middle of my sentence. Every single time.

Something inside of me had fundamentally shifted, and I no longer felt hurt or angry with her and what I would have interpreted as a rejection just a few months previously. Instead, I was free. I took responsibility for what I could be responsible for and let go of what wasn't my responsibility.

I no longer felt victimized by how she mothered me or angry about what was missing from her mothering. I no longer felt rejected. I no longer felt bad about how she responded to me. I was at peace and completely okay with her choice not to see me. If her dying wish was for me to not be involved in the end of her life, then I could open-heartedly give her what she wanted.

For the first time, I understood why she hung up on me. Instead of only seeing my pain, I could see the bigger picture of her life as well. I was filled with compassion for her suffering and how she must have felt hurt that I didn't let her be my mother in the only way she knew how.

I let go and I asked my brother if he would give me some time with her after she died, and he agreed. My brother called me letting me know it was getting close to our mother's passing. He told me that if I wanted to see her, then I could sit in his living room and wait for her to take her last breath.

I declined.

I was not willing to sit in a room next to my dying mother with a wall between us and decided instead to go camping and float on a raft down the river the next morning.

I asked my brother to ask our mom one last time if she wanted to see me. He called back twenty minutes later with the green light. I dropped everything and even left my tent at the campsite. I drove two hours to his home, went inside, and got into bed with my mother where I whispered softly, "I love you" repeatedly until she peacefully died in my arms nineteen hours later.

The love between my mother and me was always there. It was there even when I couldn't see it and even when I wasn't loved the way I wanted to be loved by her.

The bond between us wasn't broken by her death. My mother lives through me. I walk by a mirror and see her in my posture, in the way I walk, and in my own eyes looking back at me. I feel the ferocity of her love when I hold my own children and grandchildren. My heart is tenderized and open and I feel only kindness when thinking about her or wearing her jewelry that I now easily and joyfully adorn myself with.

The meaning we make and the interpretations we give to events, circumstances, and other people's behaviors are what determines our experience. What someone does to us can feel very personal, and it's normal to feel victimized by other people's behavior. However, taking things personally feeds victimization and gets in the way of creating the life we want. To get free, we have to let go.

Gap Work: Letting Go

Some of us think holding on makes us strong, but sometimes it is letting go.
~Hermann Hesse

Get your journal. Set your timer for fifteen minutes and answer the following question:

What do I most need to let go of?

Write about the impact of holding on and what it would feel like if you truly let go.

Tendency for Interpersonal Victimhood

The dream doesn't lie in victimization or blame; it lies in hard work, determination, and good education.
~Alphonso Jackson

Feeling victimized makes it difficult to let go whereas understanding how you're living in victimization makes it easier to let go. For most of my adult life, I felt victimized not just by my mother but also by most of my interpersonal relationships. The tendency to feel victimized by other people, especially those closest to us has been identified by researchers as a Tendency for Interpersonal Victimhood (TIV).[7]

Let's look at what TIV is so you will know if, and when, you're experiencing it. No shame, okay?

The Tendency for Interpersonal Victimhood is feeling like a victim most of the time in many different relationships. There are four areas of interpersonal victimhood:

1. A need for recognition.
2. Moral elitism.
3. Lack of empathy.
4. Rumination.

While reviewing each of these areas, keep in mind that awareness is a key to changing tendencies and habits.

A Need for Recognition

The first area of the Tendency for Interpersonal Victimization is the need for recognition. You'll know you have a need for recognition if you tell your story repeatedly to get empathy and acknowledgment for how you were victimized. It doesn't matter what happened, it always feels like someone else is doing you wrong.

---

[7] https://www.gwern.net/docs/psychology/personality/2020-gabay.pdf

The need for recognition is an unconscious way we try to gain compassion and support from others. Telling our story from a victimized perspective comes from trying to make sense of the world around us and to gain acknowledgment for how much we're hurting.

While the need for recognition is understandable, continuing to grasp for recognition from a victimized perspective will only concretize your victimization. You can learn healthy and non-victimized ways to acknowledge your pain.

When you first tell your story, you may need to acknowledge all the ways you were victimized. Certainly, I was deeply hurt by both of my parents. However, telling the story over and over only deepened my victimization and got in the way of my taking responsibility for my adult life. I was more committed to how I was hurt in the past than I was to what I wanted to create in my future.

For now, notice if you tend to tell your story in a way to gain recognition and empathy. Then you can work with a therapist to learn how to share your story from a place of personal responsibility and what you want to create for yourself and those you love.

Moral Elitism

The second area of the Tendency for Interpersonal Victimization is moral elitism. You can know you're experiencing moral elitism if you're holding onto a positive self-image while judging others as being immoral, unfair, or selfish. Engaging in moral elitism is a way of getting away from painful feelings but doing so only keeps you stuck in victimization.

The anecdote to moral elitism is vulnerability. You can free yourself from moral elitism by learning how to assess yourself more accurately without comparing or judging others and then vulnerably sharing with others.

Lack of Empathy

The third area of the Tendency for Interpersonal Victimization is a lack of empathy, which is a preoccupation with your own suffering that leads to feeling entitled to behave in ways that lack empathy for others. Minimizing others' suffering while bringing attention to yours will never free you of victimization.

The anecdote for a lack of empathy is finding compassion for yourself and others.

Rumination

Last, those who have the Tendency for Interpersonal Victimization ruminate excessively on problems and offenses inflicted on them while avoiding looking for solutions. One way you can know you're stuck in rumination is if you blame everything which isn't working for you today on what happened to you when you were a child. Blaming the past can sound like this:

If only..., then...

- If only I had better parents, then...
- If only I wasn't sexually abused, then...
- If only they treated me better, then...

The anecdote for rumination is to stop connecting what happened in the past with what you're currently experiencing. While the abuse does have an impact on your life, you can get free of the impact by looking for solutions to what's happening today instead of ruminating on the problems of the past.

Gap Work: Do You Have a Tendency for Interpersonal Victimhood?

*As you embrace this idea that you own your life,
you begin to exercise dominion over it.
~Amy Leigh Mercree*

The Tendency for Interpersonal Victimhood is normal but doesn't leave us with personal power or a sense of satisfaction in our relationships. Remember, awareness is key to making changes, so don't worry if you discover you have a Tendency for Interpersonal Victimhood—becoming aware is a step in the right direction.

Here are questions used in researching the Tendency for Interpersonal Victimhood, which captures the essence of the four areas. Let's see where you stand. Rate how much you agree with each of these items on a scale of one (not me at all) to five (this is so me):

1. It's important to me for people who hurt me to acknowledge that an injustice has been done to me.
2. I think I'm much more conscientious and moral in my relationships with other people compared to their treatment of me.
3. When people who are close to me feel hurt by my actions, it's very important for me to clarify where justice is on my side.
4. It's very hard for me to stop thinking about the injustices others have done to me.

What did you discover? Share your insights in your journal.

If what you've found feels vulnerable, then you're on the right track. You have reason to rate yourself as you have. Who wouldn't want an acknowledgment from the person who harmed them and the impact it has had on their life and relationships?

Regarding being sexually abused, you're justified in thinking you're more conscientious and moral in your relations with others. There was no morality in how the person harmed you. It was wrong. Period. It makes sense that you would be extra sensitive to hurting others and wanting to make sure the person who feels hurt by you understands why you did what you did.

Since change begins with awareness, you must be conscious of being stuck in victimization before you can get free. The Tendency for Interpersonal Victimhood is normal given what you've lived through. However, victimization can bleed into all areas of your life and all relationships. It's quite common to grow up feeling like a victim far into adulthood. Why? Because this habit was established in early childhood with primary caregivers. It's not your fault, but it's your responsibility to deal with today.

We'll look at some of the ways victimization solidifies the feeling of victimization, making it difficult to shake and get free. I can guide you, but you're the only one who can free yourself from continuing to live from a victimized perspective.

I found my way out of victimization through learning how to be vulnerable with myself and others. It takes a lot to change, but with the right tools, support, and awareness, you can get free too.

The first meeting with a coach or therapist includes sharing your story. You need to let them know why you're hiring them and what you want to change in your life. In the beginning, representing yourself as a victim is normal.

> My client, Amber, knew she was embedded in victimization but couldn't get free from its debilitating grip.
>
> Amber repeated her story week after week of how wronged she was by everyone and everything. She shared that no matter how hard she worked it was never enough. People were always doing something which made her feel she wasn't good enough.
>
> When her client changed jobs and lost the ability to authorize a significant purchase order, Amber questioned her client's morality for not making the purchase a priority before changing jobs. After all,

Amber thought, "I made plans for that money. They should have thought of that before they took another job."

Amber ruminated over how nothing ever went her way. She had a hard time forgiving herself and others. The experiences in her life left her feeling angry, disappointed, and upset with herself and others.

Amber's unprocessed anger colored every part of her life, especially her work where she strived for perfection and constantly judged everyone around her as not being good enough. She lost many clients who complained of her as acting righteous and standoffish.

Amber's victimization was a result of early childhood trauma where she felt she wasn't good enough. Her belief compelled her to strive for perfection and anything less led her to intense judgment. Amber turned every complaint her clients had into an attack on their integrity.

Amber's life started changing once she recognized her inability to be vulnerable around her own human imperfections and started sharing her real self with me and eventually with the people closest to her. Today, Amber is completely free of victimization. She correctly interprets her early wounding as having nothing to do with her value as a worthy human being. She's kind and compassionate with herself and others. Today, she has a thriving business in which her clients adore and respect her.

The Tendency for Interpersonal Victimization is an unconscious reaction to the trauma experienced in early life. If you have a Tendency for Interpersonal Victimization, then it's not your fault, but it's yours to handle and figure out.

Culture of Victimization

*I am not what I think I am, and I am not what you
think I am. I am what I think you think I am.
~Charles Horton Cooley*

Socialization is the process of learning to behave in ways that are acceptable to society. We live in a culture that encourages victimization and in which individuals tend to avoid taking personal responsibility. A culture of victimization is created in two ways. First, we're socialized to not take responsibility for what we've done. Second, we're socialized to blame others. What's acceptable and unacceptable becomes clear to a young child. For example, when one child hurts another, parents will often demand in an angry or accusatory tone, "Why did you do that? Say you're sorry!" Since it's unacceptable to hurt other people, denying wrongdoing to avoid punishment appears to be a better option than admitting the truth and taking responsibility for the harm you caused.

It's uncomfortable to accept responsibility for causing harm. The person who caused harm may attempt to redirect the attention from themselves by blaming the person they harmed or by changing the topic. This unconscious tactic to take the pressure off oneself is part of our socialization to avoid responsibility.

Another tactic to avoid responsibility is the tendency to want to apologize quickly and move on. We're socialized to say "sorry" to get out of trouble, not because we feel sorry for what we've done or because we feel empathy or compassion toward who we've harmed. Empathy and compassion are qualities which develop through thoughtful contemplation of the impact someone's behavior has on another person.

While apologizing is an appropriate response after hurting someone, bypassing the contemplation phase leaves us saying sorry to avoid responsibility—not to take responsibility. We can develop empathy by taking time to think about the impact our actions have on others. We can teach empathy by guiding children to think about what they've done and asking questions like: "Johnny is crying; how do you think he feels about you hitting him?" This type of question requires the person who did harm to step inside of someone else's experience whereas the demand for an apology bypasses thoughtful consideration and doesn't teach empathy.

When the threat of punishment increases, so does the avoidance of responsibility. The bigger the punishment, the more likely a person is to become defensive, deny, give excuses, make justifications, and lie when they're confronted with doing something wrong. Like all members of society, sexual offenders are socialized to lie. They know their actions are wrong but can't get help without losing everything.

Because of how society views convicted sexual offenders, they're at greater risk of self-harm and suicide than any other types of convictions. They're also at high risk of being harmed by other people in prison. Without professional support and resources to get the help they need, sexual offenders will find it difficult to get help in taking responsibility for what they've done. The stakes are just too high.

We don't consciously allow abuse to continue, but our current methods for dealing with sexual abuse aren't stopping abuse from happening; instead, they push the shame around sexual offending deeper into the shadow, making it near impossible for the person who did harm to tell the truth, take responsibility, or make an amends.

If the presenter I shared earlier where 500 women were asked to stand if they had been sexually abused had also asked the people who had sexually abused someone to stand, I doubt anyone would have stood up. Yet, statistically, there's an abuser for every one of the people in that room who remained standing—there had to have been sexual offenders in that room also. How do we get the sexual offenders to stand up and take responsibility the way my father did?

We can't end sexual abuse until we understand how it's created—where it starts. As a society, we need to value the truth more than we despise sexual offenders, which is a difficult thing to ask an individual, let alone an entire society. Our society can begin to end childhood sexual abuse and build a safe world for our children by socializing children to tell the truth because it's the right thing to do.

While this book is written for survivors of childhood sexual abuse, it's also for sexual offenders who are willing to take full responsibility for what they've done and for the impact of their actions. Those who have caused harm need healing too. The tendency to dehumanize sexual offenders won't get us any closer to stopping abuse. Relating to people as villains who have done harm won't end sexual abuse. We need to make *abuse* the problem and humanize the people impacted by including survivors, family members, the larger community, and *sexual offenders*.

While it's the individual who offends, we tend to think sexual abuse would end if the individual who causes harm would stop. It's a much more complex issue than we want to believe, and we can't end childhood sexual abuse without a comprehensive understanding of the many contributing factors. Tragically, one of the reasons people harm others is because of their own early childhood wounding. Only by including offenders and what happened to them, will we be able to finally understand the complex dynamics which precipitate abuse.

Growth and recovery can be enhanced by understanding the bigger societal picture of sexual offending. As difficult as it might be to relate to the offender as someone who deserves compassion and consideration, we need to include offenders if we are to find a workable solution that ends the behavior.

Victimization and Blame

> *When you blame others,*
> *you give up your power to change.*
> *~Robert Anthony*

While people want to know why life isn't going their way, most resort to blame instead of taking responsibility for their future. Blaming the person who hurt you for what's happening in your life today is understandable and can temporarily feel good, but blame won't get you out of victimization.

The following exercise is designed to raise your awareness of who and what you're blaming people for so you can take another step toward freedom.

Gap Work: Blame Dump

> *Tell your secret to the wind, but don't blame it for*
> *telling the trees.*
> *~Khaled Hosseini, A Thousand Splendid Suns*

Get out your journal. In this exercise you're encouraged to blame everything and everyone else for what isn't working in your life today. This is an awareness building exercise and isn't a time to censor yourself or take responsibility for anything.

Set the timer for five minutes and complain about everything that has been done to you. Remember, don't take any responsibility for why your life is the way it is.

Here are some questions to get you started:

- Who or what am I blaming for the condition of my life?
- What am I complaining about? Whose fault is it?
- What never goes my way? Why?
- What do I believe shouldn't be happening? Who caused what's happening?
- What circumstances do I seem unable to change? Whose fault is it?
- Why do I think everything is happening the way it is?

After the timer rings answer these questions:

1. What did I notice?
2. How much am I blaming others for the condition of my life today?

It's difficult to create a healthy fulfilling life if all the available energy is going toward blaming someone. An important aspect of healing is to acknowledge the abuse, let go of making anyone else responsible for what's happening today, and take responsibility for your own healing and transformation in the present.

It can be challenging to include both the truth of what someone did and, at the same time, take responsibility for what happens after the abuse. Some common complaints years after the abuse ended includes:

- Having an unhealthy codependent relationship.
- Alcohol or drug addiction (self or partner).
- Not being able to set clear consistent boundaries.
- Feeling unsafe.
- Feeling powerless and unable to create a happy, healthy life or relationship.

Upleveling your understanding of who's responsible for your life today can restore your power. The reason a person doesn't get free of the impact of abuse isn't because of the abuse, it's because they haven't learned how to get free of the impact of the abuse *in the present*.

Whatever happens in your adult life after the abuse is your responsibility no matter how horrific the actions inflicted upon you were. While you might not be able to stop the trajectory of its impact on your current life overnight, getting help today will have a significant positive impact on your future.

Self-Victimization

> *You can send a man to hell,*
> *but you can't make him suffer.*
> ~George Hammond

Any victimization a survivor of abuse is experiencing today is happening in their own mind. To stop being a victim of something which happened in the past, you must become aware of how you're victimizing yourself in the present, or how you're setting yourself up to be victimized by others in the future.

Gap Work: Self-Victimization

> *We live in a society of victimization, where people*
> *are much more comfortable being victimized than*
> *actually standing up for themselves.*
> ~Marilyn Manson

To get free of the impact of abuse, you must be honest with how you keep your victimization alive today. Get out your journal and identify how you're victimizing yourself.

Self-victimization can sound like this:

- I can't do it because...
- They always...
- This always happens to me.
- I can't say anything.
- You don't understand.

Make a list of how you victimize yourself in the above ways. Pay attention to the dialogue you have with yourself over the next few days and add to your list.

Self-victimization is an avoidance of personal responsibility and can show up as an experience of:

- Procrastination.
- Apathy.

- Playing small and not living to your potential or overachieving while feeling inadequate.
- Not taking advantage of opportunities to learn new skills.
- Staying in unsatisfying relationships.
- Resentment and anger toward others for how they treat you, but not changing it.

Make a list of all the choices you're making to avoid taking personal responsibility for your life.

A key indicator if you're living inside of victimization is if you hear yourself say, "My life is this way because of what happened to me." To get out of victimization you must stop giving power to the past. What happened, happened. It's true; it happened. But your life is the way it is because of the choices *you've* been making.

The choices you make affect your life in many ways. To get free of the impact of abuse, make a list of the new conscious choices you need to start making. Ask yourself the following questions:

- What do I need to start doing?
- What do I need to stop doing?
- What support do I need to make sure I start making the choices I know will give me the results I want?

Child vs. Adult Thinking—Simple vs. Complex

The ideal art, the noblest of art: working with the complexities of life...
~Joyce Carol Oates

In abusive situations, children have no control over what happens to them. When abuse is present, children abandon themselves and align with their caregivers. A child holding abusive adults responsible threatens the child's survival as they're completely dependent on their caregivers to provide everything they need. It's often safer for children to blame themselves for the abuse which happened to them than to make their caregivers wrong.

Adapting to our early environment is a brilliant, intuitive survival strategy, which stops working in adulthood. Adult survivors of abuse develop additional strategies to keep themselves safe, like trying to control every aspect of their daily life. Micromanaging the world doesn't really work, however. While it's an attempt to create safety, habitual obsessive behaviors are only an illusion of control—it's the unconscious habits that are in control.

The reality is you can't control most of what happens to you in life. The reality is most of what happens in life has nothing to do with what happened to you as a child. Good things are going to happen. Bad things are going to happen. So, what do you have control over?

- You have control over the meaning you make about what happens.
- You have control over the actions you take and how you respond.
- You have control over raising your consciousness to access your power to grow.

Adults have the capacity to think with complexity. For example, adults are able to discern that they are loved by some people, but not all people. In contrast, children think in simple terms, i.e., either I'm loved or I'm unloved. You'll know you're in your adult mind when you can hold two conflicting ideas at the same time. For example:

- A person can do bad things, but it doesn't make them bad.
    The child believes, "I AM bad."

- Two people can be right about something at the same time.
    The child believes, "I'm right and you're wrong." Or "I'm wrong and you're right."

- You're not responsible for what happened to you, and you're fully responsible for how you respond to what happened to you.
    The child believes, "It's all my fault."

When the thinking which was present when the abuse happened doesn't get updated, then the simple all-or-nothing child perspective gets collapsed into our adult experience making it difficult to differentiate the past from the present. With the child and adult consciousness enmeshed, the belief we created about ourselves as a child will feel very true far into adulthood.

A core component to the healing process and accessing personal power is learning how to hold several different perspectives at the same time. It's your responsibility, as an adult, to dismantle the trap between the child and adult perspectives that keeps you victimized and powerless to get free of the impact of the abuse.

Here's an example of enmeshment of the past and present:

If you have a belief that you're unworthy because of the abuse, then you're in the limited perspective of the child. If it *feels* true that you're unworthy, even when you logically know better, then your child and adult perspectives are enmeshed.

Learning how to hold complexity will alleviate pain. The adult truth is the abuse had NOTHING to do with you. The adult truth is that your worthiness is not connected to your being abused or not. The adult truth is you didn't have the capacity to think like the adult you are today.

It's more painful to make the abuse mean you are unworthy than to interpret the abuse through a more sophisticated adult lens such as:

- The abuse was not personal to me.
- The fact someone abused me doesn't mean there is anything wrong with me or that I'm unlovable, unworthy, or bad.
- The person who hurt me did something wrong and bad to me.

Gap Work: Child vs. Adult Thinking

Simplicities are enormously complex.
Consider the sentence, "I love you."
~Richard O. Moore, Writing in Silences

Most people have a difficult time accessing their adult thinking when referring to themselves. If it's difficult for you to access what's true today, then imagine there's another child the same age as you were sitting in front of you.

Get out your journal and answer these questions:

- What childlike interpretations am I making about the abuse?
- What is the truth about each of the interpretations I made?

Taking Responsibility for Your Relationships

There is an expiry date on blaming your parents for steering you in the wrong direction; the moment you are old enough to take the wheel, responsibility lies with you.
~J.K. Rowling

Do you have unhealthy adult relationships because of what happened to you as a child?

You learn how to be in relationships by observing early caregivers and witnessing the relationships around you. However, the past doesn't have to limit your future.

Getting free of abuse requires you to hold complexity to understand that whatever you experienced has an impact on your choices *and* you're the one responsible for getting help to learn how to be in relationship with others in healthy ways. You only need to know it's your responsibility to stop using what happened in early childhood as the reason for not having the kinds of relationships you want today, and your life will start changing.

You can be impacted by past abuse, and at the same time, you can get free of the ways abuse still haunts you today. Even if there are consistent negative habitual patterns in your current relationships which keep getting recreated, you can get free.

I had a pivotal experience with my father illustrating that what I'm teaching you works.

> I made plans to make a birthday dinner for my father. As a special surprise, I secretly invited family members to join us. When my father didn't show up for dinner at the agreed upon time, I called him to make sure he was okay. Instead of telling me he was running a little

late, he informed me he had changed plans and would be celebrating his birthday with friends instead of having dinner with me.

I felt an old familiar sting of believing I didn't matter enough for him to even make a simple phone call. With a hurting heart, I revealed the surprise to him. Once he knew several of his family members were waiting for him, he immediately agreed to come home.

As soon as I hung up the phone, tears started flowing and I caught myself reciting the old familiar mantra, *See, it's true. I don't matter.*

Having recognized this as my core false belief, I stopped myself mid-tear and realistically assessed the situation from my adult self instead of the hurt child.

Was it true that I didn't matter?

Nope. Even if he treated me like I didn't matter, it wasn't true.

So, I told myself the highest truth. I reassured myself, "Sweetheart, you matter to ME! That's bad behavior on your father's part."

Being connected to myself and inside the truth of my own mattering, I felt strong and stable and clear and centered in my adult self—taking care of the part of me that felt hurt.

When my father arrived, I stayed in my adult center. I didn't slam doors; I didn't toss around pots and pans to passive-aggressively show everyone how hurt I felt; I wasn't sarcastic; I didn't sulk or punish my father in any way. I graciously and authentically greeted my father when he arrived and celebrated his birthday joyfully with our family.

I didn't let his bad behavior go either.

The next day, I had an adult heart-to-heart conversation with my father letting him know he's welcome to celebrate his birthday dinner, or any dinner, in any way he chooses. It never has to be with me. However, it's not possible for him to break his agreements with me while keeping a special place as one of the important people I choose to prioritize in my life.

I explained with open-hearted clarity that I don't let people who blow me off stay close to me, even my father. I let my father know that if he wanted to remain in my closest circle, then he must do better. My father immediately apologized and took full responsibility for his bad behavior and made a commitment to never treat me like that again. He kept his promise to me.

If you would have told me forty years ago that I would have this kind of adult conversation and relationship with my father, I would have said you were crazy. I didn't blame him or shame him. I didn't make myself wrong. I simply took responsibility for changing my patterns and let him know what I needed from him.

The hard emotional work I've done to engage in this type of adult behavior was made possible through my work with Katherine Woodward Thomas. Her True You Awakening process, which I specialize in, helps people deconstruct their false beliefs and take responsibility for how they relate to themselves and the world around them. Go to my website to learn more about the True You Awakening process and how it can help you.

Now, let's take another step forward.

Gap Work: Relationship Responsibility

Everybody is responsible for their own actions. It's easy to point the finger at somebody else, but a real man, a real woman, a real person knows when it's time to take the blame and when to take responsibility for their own actions.
~Marcus Smart

Get out your journal and make a list of relationships which don't work.

For each relationship:

- Describe what keeps happening.
- In what ways do I feel disappointed or let down in each relationship?
- What do I most want to change in each relationship?

Notice any similarities or patterns that are consistent in all the relationships. Include patterns of how you're treated and how you feel.

Taking Responsibility for What Is Yours

Everything can be taken from a man but one thing: the last of the human freedoms—to choose one's attitude in any given set of circumstances, to choose one's own way.
~Victor Frankl

The truth is that you were victimized, but you don't have to live your life inside of victimization. You can create something new and beautiful completely outside of whatever happened to you. The quality of your life changes when you choose to step out of victimization and take responsibility for what's truly yours. Taking responsibility becomes easier when you're able to discern the ways you're both avoiding taking responsibility and taking responsibility for what belongs to someone else.

Gap Work: Taking Responsibility

Thinking for yourself and making your own decisions can be frightening. Letting go of other people's expectations can leave you feeling empty for a time. And yet seeing yourself as an independent adult who can stand up for your own choices frees you to accept yourself as you are.
~Ellen Bass, The Courage to Heal: A Guide for Women Survivors of Child Sexual Abuse

Knowing what is and isn't yours to take responsibility for may take considerable self-reflection, so get out your journal. It's time to identify where you're avoiding taking responsibility.

There are many ways people don't take responsibility. You can identify a shirking of responsibility when you're engaging in blaming others for the condition of your life, complaining without taking effective action, or not getting the help you need to grow.

Here are some common ways of not taking responsibility for what *is* yours:

- Avoiding taking the initiative to move your life in the direction you want it to go in.
- Not prioritizing what matters to you.
- Blaming others for your mistakes or shortcomings.
- Not taking care of your body, including nourishment and exercise.
- Engaging in negativity.

Make a list of the ways you avoid taking responsibility for what is yours:

Now that you see clearly what you're avoiding taking responsibility for, make a list of what you are willing to take responsibility for.

An equally harmful behavior is to take responsibility for what isn't yours. The most common way people identify if someone is being overly responsible is if they engage in codependent behaviors.

Some ways you can recognize if you're taking responsibility for what *isn't* yours is if:

- You solve problems that aren't yours to solve.
- You do things for others that they can do for themselves.
- You change your behavior when you think it will upset someone.
- You believe what someone does to you is your fault.

Taking responsibility for someone's feelings of frustration, resentment, or anger is a no-win situation. If you try to be responsible for how others interpret what you say or do, then you'll walk on eggshells trying to avoid hurting them.

Make a list of the ways you take responsibility for what isn't yours.

Now write one way you're willing to stop taking responsibility for something that isn't yours:

You can always stop taking responsibility for:

- Any abuse that happened to you.
- Other people's healing.

Part Six
Understanding Sexual Offending

*We can't solve problems by using the same kind of
thinking we used when we created them.
~Albert Einstein*

Sexual offending is possible in part because of the forces that contribute to how we, as a society, unconsciously allow sexual abuse to continue. These forces include the following factors:

- The shame we tend to feel around sexual abuse—survivor and offender alike.
- The discomfort we feel around having an open dialogue about sexual abuse with survivors, offenders, and those who are vulnerable to being sexually abused.
- The ways culture accepts patriarchy.
- The ways we are and have been socialized to accept sexual abuse in our media and where we exploit children's innocence.
- Not understanding the role an individual plays in a family.
- A lack of education on recidivism and restoration.

To start understanding the process of sexual offending and how society and individuals play a role in childhood sexual abuse, let's look at what you currently believe about childhood sexual abuse.

Gap Work: Personal Beliefs

I need one of those long hugs where you kinda forget whatever else is happening around you for a minute.
~Marilyn Monroe

Get out your journal. Set aside thirty minutes to answer the following questions and journal about what you know and believe about people who sexually abuse children.

- What are my beliefs about people who sexually abuse children?
- What should happen to people who sexually abuse children?
- How many types of sexual offenders are there? What are the differences between them?
- What do I think contributes to how I think sex offenders should be dealt with?
- What do I think makes sexual abuse possible in a society that despises it so much?
- How has having been harmed by sexual abuse impacted what I believe about people who sexually abuse children?

There's no good reason for why some people sexually abuse their children. The why for me became much clearer when I had access to research done by Sabrina Trobak during her training with the Yellowhead Family Sexual Abuse Treatment Program, one of the first programs that works with the entire family healing from sexual abuse. When I shared the following section with my father, he broke down in tears in recognition of himself as a sexually regressed offender. Finally, he had a name for why he hurt me, and this understanding brought us both additional freedom.

Depending on your personal circumstances surrounding the abuse you experienced, you may also find comfort. Either way, it's better to be aware of the type of sexual offender who harmed you, so you can make smart choices for you and your family.

Types of Sexual Offenders

We deserve to have our wrongdoing represented as much as our heroism, because when we refuse wrongdoing as a possibility for a group of people, we refuse their humanity.
~Carmen Maria Machado, In the Dream House

The traditional classification of sex offenders is inadequate in addressing treatment and recidivism. Because of a lack of education, we tend to relate to all offenders the same. But they aren't the same, nor do they deserve the same treatment.

The Office of Sex Offender Sentencing, Monitoring, Apprehending, Registering, and Tracking (SMART) focuses on adult offenders and the different types of sexual offenders and advocates for providing resources and understanding offense patterns and risk. Statistics show that whether someone will repeat their behavior is determined by the type of sexual offender they are.

You're probably unaware "the most important distinction among child sexual abusers [in predicting recidivism] is whether they are pedophiliac or non-pedophiliac"[8] offenders. Understanding this difference can help you make a choice for you and your family about whether to include the person who caused the harm in your healing process. The foundational difference between the two is in sexual preference and attraction.

- Pedophilia is defined as someone who has a sexual preference for children, even if the preference doesn't result in sexual abuse.
- The non-pedophile is sexually attracted to adults.

While I can help most survivors of childhood sexual abuse because they have similar post-abuse experiences regardless of the type of sexual offender who caused them harm, advocating for every type of sexual offender is beyond the

---

[8] Hanson & Bussiere, 1998

scope of this book and my expertise. My focus is on the regressed sexual offender, who "knows what he's doing is wrong, feels guilt and wants to stop abusing the child... With in-depth, long-term, proper treatment, regressed sex offenders can overcome this behavior."[9]

The *regressed sexual offender* is a non-pedophiliac offender. They "offend because of blurred boundaries and maladaptive coping strategies for dealing with stress, not because of a predisposed sexual attraction to children."[10]

My father was a regressed sexual offender. He received in-depth, long-term, and expert therapy, which resulted in his taking full responsibility for the harm he caused. He made a powerful intention to end the cycle of abuse with him, and he was successful.

Understanding what led up to the abuse helped me relate to my father as a person who was also harmed as a child and had difficulty coping in his adult life. My abuse was, in part, an impact of *his* early childhood abuse. Becoming aware of what motivated him to hurt me opened the door to his own healing and helped him gain clarity on what could cause a regression. Being able to recognize and avoid situations that left him feeling the way he did when he was a kid made it possible for him to stay present to any potential dangers and avoid re-offending altogether. He was courageous and vigilant in staying awake. My father's successful repair gives me hope for other regressed sexual offenders, their families, and the potential for ending this type of abuse.

My father and I spoke openly with each other about the abuse. It became progressively easier to have difficult conversations with him over the years. At various times I shared concerns with my father after witnessing him navigate difficult life circumstances. He always listened and took my concerns seriously. On occasion, we met with a therapist to make sure the foundation of our healing stayed strong and to ensure the continued safety in our family and community. Learning how family dynamics contribute to abuse gave me confidence about the choices I made around having my father present in my children's lives.

---

[9] Trobak, 2011

[10] Martens, 1988

The Roles We Play

People who are crazy enough to think they can change the world are the ones who can do it.
~Steve Jobs

A thoughtful, albeit uncomfortable, understanding of the roles we play in making sexual abuse possible in our society may help in ending childhood sexual abuse.

The truth is *everyone* plays a role including police departments, investigators, teachers, parishioners, parents, caregivers, siblings, friends, yourself, *and* the one taking the action to abuse others. Whether it's through your indifference, discomfort with the topic, or quickness to blame the offender, we all play a role in keeping the system in place as it is.

Tony Martens developed one of the first, and few, programs that offer treatment instead of incarceration for sexual offenders. Sabrina Trobak's research, "Families of Sexual Abuse: The Roles Each Member Plays," shows the process on how sexual abuse by the regressed sexual offender happens. If you want a comprehensive understanding of the relational dynamics surrounding the regressed sexual offender, then I highly recommend you visit my website and read the entire article.

Here's a synopsis:

Step 1: Where there are difficulties in the relationship, the family is vulnerable to abuse.

- Father does not have a sexual attraction to children.
- Father does not plan for sexual abuse to happen.
- Father does not feel loved by his partner, but he does feel loved by his daughter.
- Mother is resentful and angry toward her daughter and jealous of the love between her daughter and her husband.

Step 2: How each family member plays an unconscious role in the potential for abuse to happen.

Father

- Father shows up in nurturing and caring ways.
- The first sexual interaction between father and daughter is accidental.
- Father is surprised by being aroused.
- Daughter does not know initially that he is sexually aroused.
- Mother is in the room, but unaware of the incidental touching from father to daughter.
- Father's stress leads to fighting with his wife creating more distance from each other, driving him to daughter for comfort.
- Because of the connection he feels to his daughter, father is drawn to her and abuses her again.
- Daughter senses arousal but does not truly understand.
- Daughter is confused that her mother doesn't stop the touching and stops trusting mother to keep her safe.
- Father is angry with himself and feels shame.
- Father's stress leads to more conflict with wife then abusing his daughter again; his stress goes down.
- Father feels connected with daughter and at the same time does his best to make sure that his daughter doesn't tell by separating her from the rest of the family, threatening her if she does tell, and/or treating her really well.

Mother

- Mother feels jealous of her daughter's connection with father and pushes her daughter away.
- Mother feels stressed because of what she senses is happening between her husband and her daughter and separates herself from the family even more.
- Daughter feels this distancing as an abandonment by her mother and feels resentful.
- Mother goes to the doctor for her physical ailments and stress and may be admitted to the hospital.
- Daughter perceives her mother as being weak (or not strong enough to handle the information), so she doesn't tell her mother about the abuse.

Sibling

- Sibling feels they don't fit in; they feel they are missing out on the connection, love, and care they see happening between the sister and father.

- Sibling starts to feel angry and resentful toward their sister.
- Sibling feels confused if they find out about the abuse. They internalize not being abused to mean they weren't good enough.
- Sibling is often left out of therapy, which may lead them to feel invisible.

Daughter/Victim

- Daughter's relationship with her family become troubled, and she feels her father is the only one who is there for her.
- When the abuse first happens, daughter goes into a freeze trauma response, then later blames herself.
- Daughter believes the abuse was a one-time thing, but when it happens again she is dumfounded and feels stuck and unable to tell.
- Daughter feels an enormous amount of guilt and shame, ensuring her silence.
- Daughter separates herself from the world to prevent herself from telling anyone about the abuse; she slips into a sense of deep loneliness, afraid and alone.
- Daughter is terrified of her family breaking apart and continues to keep silent.

Understanding the process of sexual abuse can bring compassion to why you might not have told anyone about the abuse, or if you did tell, why you didn't get the protection you needed. Understanding how sexual abuse happens in families can help you avoid the traps that lead to sexual abuse today. Let's look at what motivates children to keep quiet.

Why Children Don't Tell

Silence by any other name is called shame.
~Shannon L. Alder

The most common reason children don't talk about sexual abuse is fear, shame, or embarrassment. Here's how fear, shame, and embarrassment are experienced:

- They don't have the words for what happened to them.
- They believe the abuse is their fault.
- They are manipulated into not telling.
- They don't want to get the person who abused them in trouble.
- They were threatened.

Children are dependent on adults for survival. Maslow's Hierarchy of Needs suggests there are unconscious reasons children don't tell. As you can see in the chart, a person's physiological and safety needs are the foundation for living a fully expressed life. If you're challenged with the higher-level needs, then work on establishing the first two and the rest will follow.

Self-Actualization Needs
Desire to become the most that one can be

Esteem Needs
Respect, self-esteem, status, recognition, strength, freedom

Love & Belonging Needs
Friendship, intimacy, family, series of connection

Safety Needs
Personal Security, employment, resources, health, property

Physiological Needs
Air, water, food, shelter, sleep, clothing, reproduction

I've been making decisions to tell or not tell for different reasons throughout my life. My decision to not tell when I was a kid fit into Maslow's safety needs listed in the above chart. In addition, I felt confused about what my father did and had an overwhelming sense of shame, believing the abuse was my fault. I worried about what would happen to me and my family if anyone found out what my father had done.

I was in the fourth grade when neighbors called the police because they heard kids screaming in our home. When the police pulled my brother and me out of school to question us without our parents knowing about whether they hit us, my brother innocently nodded his head, "Yes."

I immediately contradicted him emphatically telling the police *our parents did not hit us.* We were just rambunctious kids playing loudly. We played tag and hide-and-seek and chased each other through the house.

I had a normal fun childhood, until the abuse. Our parents were engaged with us. We played card and board games together, they took us to the park, we went camping, and we had close family friends.

Later, when the abuse was happening in the middle of our everyday traditional life, I kept silent. The instinct to protect my parents was strong. I protected my father by keeping quiet. I shut myself in my bedroom and turned away from my friends and family.

My mother knew something was going on with me and she came to my bedroom to find out. She brought my father with her, and he sat silently in a chair looking at me while my mother asked me over and over what was wrong. My father said nothing. I said nothing. It was a secret I didn't even have words for at the time. I misunderstood and believed I was responsible for keeping our family together by shutting my mouth. That's too much responsibility for any child.

Gap Work: If You Didn't Tell, Why?

One believes things because one has been conditioned to believe them.
~Aldous Huxley, Brave New World

Get out your journal.

It can be healing to know why you didn't tell.

First circle any of the reasons listed below for why you didn't tell.

- Shame.
- Feeling afraid.
- Feeling responsible whether you were told it's your fault or not.
- To protect other family members.
- Not wanting to get into trouble.
- Fear of being taken away from your family.
- Thinking nobody will believe you.
- You didn't know how.

Write in your journal what you discovered about why you didn't tell.

It wasn't easy—even as an adult—to tell. I'm grateful that my father stepped up and we both started working with a therapist, but I only confronted my father before I got married because creating safety for my future children was more important than my discomfort.

Telling can bring up many fears. Here are some both my father and I experienced:

- Fear of being blamed, hated, or rejected.
- Fear that the family members we decided to *not* tell would feel betrayed by me when they found out.
- Fear that people would lose respect for the man my father had become in their lives.

Once my father and I entered therapy, we started telling others what happened. As we told family members, we got stronger. We told my grandmother, friends, and community members. We worked with a therapist and followed the ethical guideline of "pick the option that does the least harm" each time we were faced with the choice to tell or not tell. The core issue and question we had to answer was around my father's well-being and chance of recidivism.

Gap Work: Who Should I Tell?

At any given moment, you have the power to say:
this is not how my story will end.
~Jason Miller

Whether you decide to tell or not, it's important to be aware of potential dangers. Make a list of anyone you feel *needs* to know about the abuse.

- Are you aware of children being left with the person who caused you harm?
- Is the person who caused you harm in situations where they could hurt someone?
- Who do you really want to tell but don't know how?
- Do you want to talk to the person who harmed you?

Now, take a few minutes and journal about any fears you have about telling and anything else that you're noticing.

As I mentioned earlier, deciding who to tell and when to tell was fraught with concern about the impact it would have on our family. We felt confident we had created a safe family and decided it would do more harm to tell my children, so initially we didn't tell them. It wasn't easy when I *did* tell my children years later. It all worked out in the end, but there were heartbreaking consequences as we worked through the process.

Telling My Children

Abuse is never contained to a present moment; it lingers across a person's lifetime and has pervasive long-term ramifications."
~Lorraine Nilon, Breaking Free from the Chains of Silence: A respectful exploration into the ramifications of abuse hidden behind closed doors

My father and I had gone through an intensive therapeutic process and healed our relationship by the time I had children, and I felt confident my children were safe. I believed it was unnecessary to tell my children what my father had done.

My father was a different person when I was growing up from the person my children had the privilege of knowing. I had a father who sexually abused me, whereas my kids had an ideal grandfather who had already taken full responsibility for his life and his choices. My father and I were both committed to giving my children a safe grandfather and my children grew up inside of a family that didn't act out sexual abuse. My father played with my children in healthy and non-threatening ways. He guided their development from a place of strength and integrity. As they grew older, my children sought out their grandfather's wisdom.

Unfortunately, my kids were told about the abuse without any competency or proficiency. My children adored their grandfather and were devastated when we told them what he had done. It didn't matter to them that the abuse happened over thirty years ago; their view of grandpa was shattered the moment they were told. Reconciling what he had done to me, their mother, was difficult for them, and they immediately stopped talking to their grandfather.

They each reconciled with their grandfather, but it took years to work through their disappointment, grief, and heartbreak.

Aviana

> *Someday, everything will make perfect sense. So for now, laugh at the confusion, smile through the tears, be strong and keep reminding yourself that everything happens for a reason.*
> ~John Mayer

My daughter lit up when she was around her grandfather. He took the time to get to know her—to really know her. He recognized her talents and aspirations and invested his time, energy, and resources in making sure she had access to what she loved. And then he supported her in fully being herself. He was good to her.

Not only did Aviana like her grandfather, but I believe she also needed him in her life. I believe that her late teen years were more difficult without her grandfather's guidance and friendship. Of course, my father was heartbroken by her rejection. Here's what Aviana wants to share:

> My grandfather drove a tan 4-Runner and would pick me up from school. I was eleven. He would stand outside the gate to meet me and walk with me to his car. I loved the way his car smelled; like the work he'd done that day mixed with old pastries sitting on the passenger seat.
>
> We could talk about anything we wanted to. I asked him for advice on many things going on in my life and he readily gave it—but only if I asked. The opinions he had about what I was doing in my life were expressed through his love and I could hear his advice because of the way he showed up for me.
>
> I was sixteen when my grandfather and mother told me that he had molested her when she was a kid. I just got up from the table and left and didn't speak with my grandfather for five years. I asked him not to contact me, and he didn't. I took it negatively that he didn't call or write me, but today I understand he didn't reach out to me out of respect. Even though I missed him and wanted him in my life, I couldn't reach out to him until my thinking around what he did shifted, and I could see he treated me differently than what I would expect from someone who did what he did.

My grandfather went to therapy, participated in men's groups, workshops, and seminars. He read books and listened to talks and showed up for himself. He showed up for my mother. And he showed up for me.

My mother and grandfather gave me a family who talk about the unspeakable; a family who doesn't hide from things which are shameful. I have a family who is honest and open and real because of the commitment my mother and grandfather made to themselves. I've seen firsthand you can love yourself again even if you've done something you think you'll never be able to love yourself through. I forgive my grandfather for something which was never mine to forgive him for and I do it anyway.

My grandfather died the way I want to die, surrounded by people who love him, telling him we loved him, and holding his hand when he took his last breath. My mom and several other people told me it was important to tell my grandfather what I will miss most about him, how I will remember him, and what I love most about him. Laying my head on his shoulder, holding his hand, and watching the pulse on his neck, I thought about special times with him: the train ride we took to go see my nephew when he was born, the first UFC fight we watched together, and the summer programs I often quit. My grandfather taught me how to fix a toilet and he taught me how to treat someone you love well.

He was always there for me. I told my grandfather I couldn't pick one thing I loved about him. Before he died, I told him I love *everything* about him. He was the most amazing role model, caring and kind and loving. He gave me the best version of himself that was genuinely healed, the version of himself that was authentic and hilarious. And he never once hurt me. He was my best friend, he was safety for me, and he was a home when I had no other. I'm proud of my grandfather and where I come from. As hard as it was to be there with him when he died, I didn't want to run away from his death because I've seen the incredible power of staying through love.

Life is honest if you just listen to it. You may think there's no way back from certain things, but there is. After my grandfather was gone, my family and our friends sat around the kitchen table. Not only did he give me the best grandfather in the world, but he also gave me every person in the room that day, and he did it by healing himself. He worked on himself so that he could be my grandfather and so that he could have himself back again and be happy. He did that for me.

Sergio

> *The truth is unless you let go, unless you forgive yourself, unless you forgive the situation, unless you realize the situation is over, you cannot move forward.*
> ~Steve Maraboli

You can understand logically that you're not responsible for someone else's life, but still feel responsible. One of the most painful experiences for me was letting my children be on their own healing journey. Because I had worked hard to give my children a safe grandfather, I felt entitled to them continuing to have a relationship with their grandfather after we told them what he did.

My son, Sergio, loved his grandfather and had the greatest respect a person could have for another human being. Knowing his grandfather held him in unconditional love, Sergio called his grandfather for advice and direction on a regular basis. That all changed with one sentence.

Shattered is the only way to describe what happened to my son's world when we told him what my father had done to me. Sergio stopped talking to his grandfather, and I was angry. I felt devastated. I did everything in my power to create a safe family, and it was inconceivable to me that my father and son wouldn't be in each other's lives. I wanted to fix something, but it wasn't mine to fix. I tried anyway.

I knew Sergio needed his grandfather to guide him during dark times, but it wasn't happening. Sergio would have to figure it out without his grandfather. I cried many times. I made my kids not having a relationship with their grandfather my personal failure. It's the greatest pain I have endured up to this point in my life, even more than the abuse because the abuse had been healed in my heart.

I felt righteous about my father and son having a relationship and fought for years for their reconciliation. It took a while for me to let go. Letting my kids and my father figure it out on their own was so hard for me. It was hard to let the choice to forgive or not forgive be my son's choice. I meddled. I encouraged. I believed there was no reason to tell my kids because they weren't harmed, nor were they in harm's way. I blamed others who I believed forced me to unnecessarily tell my kids what happened. I felt victimized and powerless.

I fought for my own freedom from feeling responsible for their relationship. I told myself over and over, "This is Sergio's life. My son gets to decide for himself what to do with this information." But I didn't believe it. I wanted Sergio to forgive—because *I deserved it*.

It was too painful to let the responsibility for the impact of what my father did lay on his shoulders. With support from friends, I did my best. I reminded myself over and over that it wasn't my fault they were estranged. I reminded myself, "If my father hadn't abused me, then we wouldn't be in this situation."

I also begged my father to go the extra mile and reach out to his grandson. I told my father, "If I can forgive you for what you did to me, then you can forgive Sergio for being mad at you for doing what you did to me."

My father reassured me as best he could: "This is not mother's love. I'm not doing it your way, but I love Sergio. This is grandfather's love, and if he wants what I have, then he has to come for it himself. I'll be here waiting even if it's on my deathbed."

That's when I let go of the responsibility for their relationship. Less than a year later, my son was with his grandfather on his deathbed. We gathered as a family, and it was Sergio who chose his grandfather's clothes and helped dress his lifeless body. It was Sergio who lifted his grandfather into the beautiful bamboo casket we had made for him.

After my father's death, clearing out my father's things, I found this letter that he had written to Sergio years earlier:

Dear Sergio,

We have arrived at this juncture in our relationship, which is the real birth of it. This is where each of us gets to choose the direction it goes, so here are some of the qualities I bring to the relationship: heart and compassion; openness to all of my feelings; loyalty; what you see is what you get; there are no other sides to me; I hide none! I am transparent. My heart is open to you, and you know that; I won't shut my heart off to you no matter what you do.

Our old ways of being have come to an end. At this time, I put before you a challenge and an opportunity: to continue the current ways of showing up in the world condemns Apollo [Sergio's son] and all who follow to the same shallow half-life; one father looks like the previous father. The very essence of the family which you are creating is at stake here. There is no easy path, and it is near impossible to accomplish great change alone.

So, my challenge to you is to step forward and be real with me.

Your opportunity:

I've been preparing for you and I'm ready to meet you. No bullshit allowed.

- Do you have a sense of being fulfilled?
- Are your ambitions satisfied?
- Is what you seek as reward being received?
- Are you doing your life work?
- Do you achieve only so much success?
- Are your relationships with others satisfying?

All of this and more are your birthright, but you must choose them and fight for them because the forces of everything and everyone which came before you require nothing, but by achieving these for yourself you are making it easy for the next generation.

What I see before you and me is a relationship which is changing in order to grow and mature. This is a timeless and continuous process.

Out for now.

GPa

My heartbreak is deep knowing my son and father lost ten precious years together. The missing years of wisdom and guidance still hurts me. I still pray my son will choose to learn from his grandfather's legacy on how to be the best man he can be no matter what darkness might touch him in his own life.

> *Grandfathers are just antique little boys.*
> *~Anonymous*

I asked my son, Sergio, to share his experience of his grandfather with you and he wrote this:

Secrets. My grandfather was my hero throughout my childhood and a role model in my early adult life. I mean I idolized him. He had EVERYTHING! Strong relationships, beef jerky, a bunch of nicknames, old world knowledge, skills, a riding mower, a dartboard on the front door to his house, a cool job, and a dump truck. More importantly he had time. He always had time. Time for what? Time to stop and look at the scenery, to go where I wanted, to show me how to build a bird house or a toolbox, to get a bite, to go to a yard sale, to talk on the phone, and to give advice. It didn't matter what it was, he always had time for ME in a way I had not experienced with any other person.

Nothing ever went wrong or was ever a big deal. Fender bender? We'll just fix it. Plumbing? No problem. And he could fix anything. I wanted to be just like him.

One day after spending about an hour on the phone with him, he let the cat out of the bag. He told me that when my mother was a kid, he molested her. Suddenly everything I believed in was gone.

My whole world was turned upside down and everything seemed like a lie. If he could keep this from me, how could I know what else was being kept from me? Why didn't anyone tell me? Was it all a show? I couldn't love someone who did that! To my mother!

All of who I believed my grandfather to be was suddenly replaced with anger and emptiness and *I was Alone*. Nobody had me, even if they did have me, what were *they* hiding? I covered up the emptiness and loneliness with alcohol and machismo.

I'll be fine. *I don't need anyone.* Fuck 'em!

In reality, at least with me in my lifetime, he wasn't any of the things I made up about what it meant when he told me what he had done. He wasn't some monster I made up in my mind. The healing work he and my mother had done starting before I was even born gave me the best grandfather anyone could have. I only ever knew him to be kind, generous, honest, loving, knowledgeable, goofy, and fun. My role model—someone who always had time for me. He did what he did, and he was what he was.

I'm so grateful that I got to know the man my grandfather IS. I want to be just like him.

My son had earlier heartbreaks and disappointments that left him believing he was all alone. In reaction, he pushed people away and, trying to protect himself, he disappeared into his own pain and victimization collecting evidence of his aloneness.

The healthiest living includes being responsible for what's yours and nothing else. Sergio is responsible for the meaning he makes out of what happens to him. He's responsible for staying sober and open-hearted even when he gets hurt or disappointed. He's responsible for learning how to create a life of belonging and connection even when he's scared. Sergio is collecting evidence of how deeply connected and supported he is through his choice to reach out to others, to ask for help when he needs it, and most importantly, softening his heart even though he might get hurt. I'm happy to say that today my son is living a sober life creating loving and deeply connected relationships with family and friends. I can honestly say that today, Sergio is just like all the good parts of his grandfather.

> *How we proceed with repair depends on how we remember.*
> *~Robin D. G. Kelley*

There's no easy way to tell a family member about the abuse. You might need additional preparation and help managing your expectations around what might happen after you tell.

I asked my children how I could have given them the information in a better way. Here's their advice:

- If you can, you should tell from the beginning.

My sister did tell her children from the beginning. My niece told me that she doesn't remember a time that she didn't know about the abuse. While my niece wasn't given the details of the abuse, she was given enough information to know that my father had hurt me. Knowing what happened didn't get in the way. Like my children, my niece had a wonderful relationship with her grandfather.

- If you're telling someone years after the abuse, then it's going to hurt no matter what.

It was a poor choice for me to wait until someone threatened to tell my kids. Not telling them on my terms left me feeling victimized, but more tragically, my silence put my kids into a position of having to deal with heartbreaking information when they weren't prepared for it.

In writing this book, I'm faced with the decision to tell one more time. I'm telling the whole world with the intention of honoring my experience and what I've learned so I can help you find your way out of pain and shame and back to your intrinsic wholeness. You're that important!

Now, is there someone you need to tell?

GAP WORK: Telling

> *"The potential loss of loving connection is coded by the human brain into a primal panic response."*
> *~ Dr. Sue Johnson,* Hold Me Tight

Once spoken, the secret, and the shame attached, will lose its power over you and you will discover parts of yourself that have likely been hidden since the abuse first happened. While the first several times you tell may be through trembling fears and flowing tears, the freedom that eventually comes from telling what happened is nothing less than miraculous.

Telling is not easy, but if you want freedom then telling must start somewhere. Get your journal and take some sacred time to think about who needs to know about the abuse.

Deciding who to tell is a very personal decision, so take your time to consider who you want to know. You can journal about who you would like to tell, but the most important person that needs to know what happened is *you*. So, let's focus right here with you.

- Whether this is the first time you're telling yourself what happened, or you've become comfortable sharing your story, just let everything flow through your pen onto the pages of your journal.

Have you ever thought about confronting the person who hurt you? Even if you never confront the person who hurt you, *imagining* telling them can be quite healing.

- If you're up for it, take some time to write a letter to the person who hurt you. While you may never send the letter, it can be a helpful part of the healing journey. Again, just let everything flow and write without censoring yourself.

While telling can be very cathartic, there's no reason to move faster than you're ready. This is your experience, so give yourself permission to move forward at your own pace and in your own timing.

Socialization and the Media

Thinking for yourself is still a radical act.
~Nancy Kline, Time to Think: Listening to Ignite
the Human Mind

The media is an example of how people are socialized to silently accept abuse. They play a role in desensitizing us around childhood sexual abuse by using images which exploit children's innocence to sell products. Are we outraged by these images? Or do we minimize their impact and look the other way?

Socialization: Advertising

When everyone thinks something is true, it does not make it anything more than effective marketing.
~Clifton Hill

Society doesn't provide many venues for transparency around sexuality, nor does it support authentic sexual expression and a pathway for healthy sexual development.

Our default culture tells us sex is taboo. Many religious teachings tell us abstinence is the only way, but they don't provide venues to understand how to honor our bodies as sacred. While most religious leaders are wholesome and safe people to be around, some church leaders use their power over children for their own perverted sexual satisfaction.

Most parents are uncomfortable discussing sex with their children, let alone guiding them in healthy responsible behavior around their sexuality.

Companies use sex in their advertising to sell their products.

These mixed messages are confusing for everyone, especially children who don't yet have the capacity to discern which sexual behavior is healthy and which is unhealthy. Conscious power dynamics can be quite healthy in sexual interactions. However, when there's a lack of awareness of the difference between healthy and unhealthy sexual behavior, healthy sexual expression can quickly regress into unhealthy sexual shadow behaviors including sexual abuse.

In this section are descriptions of several disturbing images that show how the media contributes to how we think about things. If you want to see the actual images, visit my website where I have them posted.

> A print advertisement is selling clothing from a well-known clothing company. It's an image of a man standing up wearing khaki-colored pants, a professional work shirt with rolled up sleeves, and a tie. You can see him from his neck to his knees. In each hand he's holding the ankles of a woman lying on her back. All you see are her legs up in the air.

Images like this exploit our sexuality and promote rape culture.

Socialization: Facts and Myths of Rape Culture

> *I look forward to the day we stop saying "me too"
> and start saying "never again."*
> *~Eva Darrows,* You Too?

On the next page is a chart showing facts and myths around rape culture in our society[11].

---

[11] Wood, 1994

Myth	Fact
Rape is a sexual act resulting from sexual urges.	Rape is an aggressive act used to dominate behavior.
Rapists are abnormal.	Rapists have not been shown to differ from non-rapists in personality, psychology, adjustment, or involvement in interpersonal relationships.
Most rapes occur between strangers.	Eighty to ninety percent of rapes are committed by a person known to the victim.
Most rapists are African American men, and most victims are Caucasian women.	More than three-fourths of all rapes occur within races, not between races. This myth reflects racism.
The way a woman dresses affects the likelihood she will be raped.	The majority—up to 90 percent—of rapes are planned in advance and without knowledge of how the victim will dress.
False reports of rapes are frequent.	The majority of rapes are never reported. Less than 10 percent of rape reports are judged false, the same as other violent crimes.
Rape is a universal problem.	The incidence of rape varies across cultures. It is highest in societies with ideologies of male dominance and a disregard for nature; it is lowest in cultures which respect women and feminine values.

Socialization: Patriarchy

You painted a naked woman because you enjoyed looking at her, put a mirror in her hand and you called the painting "Vanity," thus morally condemning the woman whose nakedness you had depicted for your own pleasure.
~John Berger, Ways of Seeing

Then we have patriarchy. Patriarchy is a system we're born into and unconsciously participate in. You can recognize patriarchy in many ways including when men hold most of the political and economic power in a society.

You may think we're far from the socialization of the '50s, but I don't think we are. We can't be free from patriarchy until we fully address the root causes and impact of patriarchy. Below is just one of the many advertisements which captures society's past acceptance of patriarchal dominance.

> In a print advertisement for coffee, a man wearing suspenders is sitting in a chair with his back to us. A woman is lying across his lap. His hand is raised to give her a spanking. The heading is, "If your husband ever finds out you're not 'store-testing' for fresher coffee."

This illustrates an unspoken patriarchal rule that men dominate and enforce rules through fear and pain We all like fresh coffee, but whose job is it to make sure it's fresh, and where does this leave children around speaking up when their own mothers are being hit for not testing the coffee for freshness? A simple internet search will reveal patriarchy, misogyny, and sexism still exist in full force today.[12]

Socialization: Exploiting Innocence in Children

No amount of me trying to explain myself was doing any good. I didn't even know what was going on inside of me, so how could I have explained it to them?
~Sierra D. Waters, Debbie

There is one advertisement from a company founded in 1974 that makes me want to vomit.

> The print advertisement is a picture of a young girl around nine years old wearing makeup and holding a Teddy Bear. The product she's selling is cologne packaged in a phallic shaped bottle. The caption reads, "Because innocence is sexier than you think."

---

[12]https://english.cofc.edu/first-year-writing/Has Our Culture Really Changed.pdf

This isn't the only advertisement this company ran that exploits children; you can still find this advertisement on YouTube:

> A young woman is sitting on the floor and dressed to appear to be about twelve years old. She has an innocent look on her face and is licking a lollipop. The caption reads: "There's one person nobody can resist, and that's a baby."

This is our culture. Disgusting!

These advertisements aired during the time I was abused, and I used this perfume that my father paid for. It's confusing to promote sexual abuse and then vilify the offender. What are they selling? With images like this, it's no surprise that so many children are sexually abused. It's in our culture. We need to acknowledge the impact advertising has on our culture, which depicts childhood sexual abuse as desirable.

What impact might this have on sexual offenders? While the offender is culpable, sexual abuse is much larger than the individual person who offends. Our laws are still catching up in holding people responsible for harming children. Until the late 19th century, children weren't even protected by law and their rights were still being ratified by Congress in the 1990s.

If you think this type of exploitation is in the past, then you'll be dismayed to know that it's not.

> A well-known sports car company posted an advertisement in 2020 of a young girl, about five years old, wearing a leopard print dress, a jean jacket, and sunglasses. She's leaning up against the front grill of a red car eating a banana. Her bent knee suggests someone who is approachable. The caption reads: "Lets your heartbeat faster—in every aspect."

While the company apologized and withdrew the add, I can't help but think, *Who are we, in our society, that anyone thought it was okay to run this advertisement in the first place?*

And yet the controversy was in full force with one view minimizing the impact of the meaning behind the images while the other was outraged. While eating a banana is a normal, non-sexual activity, it doesn't take much effort to see that these types of images promote sexual violence toward children. We can do better. We must do better.

I'm outraged.

Gap Work: What Do You Think?

Get your journal, we're going on a media field trip. Re-reading the descriptions above or viewing my website (use the QR code below and click Socialization and Media), follow these four steps for each image:

1. Consider the image (and the words).
2. Take note of how the image makes you feel.
3. Consider the impact the image has on you.
4. Write your thoughts and feelings in your journal.

Taking a Stand

How do you forgive the people who are supposed to protect you?
~Courtney Summers, Sadie

Childhood sexual abuse won't stop until we do something about it.

We can't exclusively blame sexual offenders as *the* problem within a culture that creates it. To end childhood sexual abuse, we must develop our capacity to hold the complexity of the many contributing factors, which can be confusing and cause us to believe there's only one culprit. There's not.

Culture determines what's okay and not okay. Groups of people make up culture. A higher level of responsibility is needed by society and the offender. Let's stop promoting childhood sexual abuse as one of many necessary stands we need to take. A higher level of responsibility is for us to take a stand and personally include ourselves in the effort to end childhood sexual abuse at its core.

Gap Work: If You Could Take a Stand

Get out your journal. Take about thirty minutes to write about how you would end childhood sexual abuse. What's your solution?

PS: If you were to focus on your own healing and commitment to end the cycle in your own family, that would be huge.

It's easy to engage in unhealthy relational dynamics, simply because they're familiar ways of being with each other that we rarely question in conscious ways. Let's look at how unconscious habitual ways of relating with each other can lead people to unknowingly play a role in childhood sexual abuse.

Sexual Offending and Restoration

The greater a child's terror, and the earlier it is experienced, the harder it becomes to develop a strong and healthy sense of self.
~Nathaniel Branden, Six Pillars of Self-Esteem

Not everyone who has been harmed in childhood goes on to harm others, but most everyone who does was harmed during their own childhood. A person's own childhood wounding is never a good reason to harm someone else; however, past wounding does contribute to a deeper understanding for *why* someone would hurt their own child. Underlying motivations are much more complex and, while sexual in action, the motivation isn't always sexual in nature.

Sexual abuse is a horrendous violation, but the sexual offender isn't always a monster. While everyone needs to be held accountable for their actions, a deeper understanding of the underlying factors which lead to harm being caused in the first place can be helpful. I believe sexual offenders are part of a system which has failed them. I believe they're beings who have been hurt and don't have the tools to effectively deal with their own pain.

People who cause harm are misguided human beings who are also harming themselves with the behavior they inflict on others. To stop sexual abuse, we must increase our capacity to hold two contradicting ideas at the same time.

First, there's no reason that would ever make it okay to violate another human being. Second, the wounded person who harms another also needs help to find their way back to wholeness.

What WILL stop childhood sexual abuse? Villainizing and sending sexual offenders to prison doesn't stop sexual abuse from happening. Instead, it limits our ability to gather information to understand the dynamics which lead to childhood sexual abuse in the first place.

I know how sexual abuse ended in my family. I took responsibility for the future I wanted to create and took action. I had a difficult conversation with my father and was willing to walk away from my family of origin to ensure safety in the family I was creating. While I'm grateful that my father took complete responsibility for what he did, not everyone will. It's important for you to know that you can heal without including the person who harmed you.

Throughout our healing process, I discovered my father is a good man who was wounded in childhood just like me. My willingness to include my father and his willingness to participate made our healthy adult relationship possible. His participation led him to make amends to me and our entire family and enjoy his own healing as well.

Whether it's livelihood, status, or family, the threat of loss keeps those who have caused harm from taking responsibility. Abuse can stop only when society provides a way for those who have caused harm to get help without risking losing everything they have. Owning the truth of what someone has done or taking responsibility for the impact they've had takes an enormous amount of courage, especially when there's no set, clear, and acceptable pathway for them to make amends.

Owning Up to the Truth

> *The first thing is to be honest with yourself. You can never have an impact on society if you have not changed yourself.*
> *~Nelson Mandela*

As mentioned, some sexual offenders can be helped so they don't reoffend, but they're not getting the help they need. It's important to differentiate between those who can and can't be helped. Those who are *capable* of self-reflection and change are worth investing in. Contributing to the health and well-being of certain types of offenders instead of locking them up opens the door for them to make amends for what they've done and become an advocate for others to do the same.

While the following experience is not about childhood sexual abuse, this personal story illustrates what's possible when someone takes responsibility for their actions, even when they didn't intentionally harm another being.

My friendship with Sam had a rocky start.

I met Sam in a gender-balanced workshop where sexuality could be explored inside a container that taught the value of consent and honored clearly communicated boundaries. We shared a brief romantic encounter and made plans to see each other again.

I wanted to be held and asked Sam if he would be willing to spend the night holding me without having sex. He agreed but wasn't being honest in his willingness to just hold me as I requested. Once we were tucked in for the night, he proceeded to break our agreement and his non-sexual holding turned into sexual touching.

With his mouth pressed against my neck, I tapped him on his shoulder and asked, "Do you ever want to see me again?"

Sam responded with a resounding, "Yes."

Instead of shaming him or making him wrong, I very gently and firmly reminded him of our agreement, "I'm noticing you're breaking our agreement to not be sexual tonight. If you continue to try to have sex with me, we may have a lovely evening, but certainly I will never see you again."

The clarity of my nonjudgmental communication prompted Sam to immediately stop what he was doing and keep his agreement with me—which continues to this day. Sam remains one of my best friends and most trusted cuddle buddy.

When I was getting to know Sam, he reminded me of an excited puppy, but Sam was much more than his desire. During our deepening platonic connection, I witnessed him interacting with different women, and as his friend, we talked about our individual dating experiences. I learned how much Sam adores women. I learned how he loves his enthusiasm for sex. I learned he loves variety. And I learned that Sam is polyamorous. Sam didn't know how to get what he wanted—a partner as exuberant as he was *and* the freedom to connect with other women, so he lied to the women he dated—or rather withheld his desire to be in a polyamorous relationship. His logic was he had to pretend to be monogamous because if he was honest, then women wouldn't have sex with him. He believed he could talk them into the polyamorous relationship style he wanted after they established a connection. Of course, this never happened when he was hiding the kind of sexually open relationship he longed for because it made him unsafe to the women he was dating.

It wasn't being polyamorous that made him unsafe, it was his lack of transparency, which came across to women as predatory. Being unsafe made him appear sex-starved and desperate because the monogamous women he was dating intuitively knew he was being dishonest with them and wouldn't have sex with him.

The rape accusation came after I knew Sam well enough to observe the complexity that motivated the complaint against him. The complaint sent Sam into a dark depression and at the same time on a path of self-defense and protection from a community he'd been a part of for several years.

Being accused of rape is a big deal. Just the accusation cost him his community, friendships, *some* sexuality he was enjoying, and his own dignity and self-respect.

The event took place during a workshop. I was in the room and witnessed the interaction he was accused of and clearly it wasn't rape. However, Sam couldn't acknowledge he had done anything to warrant the accusation and he fell into an automatic socialized response of defending, denying, blaming, and minimizing to avoid social rejection and serious criminal charges. Inside of the threat of a potential arrest, Sam couldn't take responsibility for how he might have contributed to the woman's perception of him and his actions.

Here's what Sam did to contribute to the accusation:

1. He chose to be sexual with someone who had been sexually abused in their childhood without talking about how to navigate potential challenges around their connection.
2. He made an agreement around the type of interaction they would have and then during the interaction pursued changing the agreement, which was very triggering for his partner.

If I hadn't healed my childhood sexual trauma, I would have felt victimized by Sam trying to be sexual with me instead of empowered to speak up and reinforce an agreement we had. Survivors who haven't healed their sexual abuse trauma can experience a freeze response when someone interacts with them sexually. This could leave their partner interpreting the trauma freeze response as consent, whereas it can leave the sexual abuse survivor feeling violated.

A man who wants to keep himself free of the accusation of rape and the sexual abuse survivor safe from feeling violated needs to keep the agreements he makes with her and stay tuned into the subtle clues which indicate consent is no longer being given.

Sexual shame hurts everyone.

On some level Sam didn't believe he could be up front about what he wanted in a sexual partner. Neither could he have what he wanted when he lied about it because the women he dated felt violated when he didn't keep his agreements.

I held Sam in love during many difficult conversations, and he finally dropped his defenses. Through compassion instead of judgment, Sam could finally see the impact he had on women when he withheld the truth of what he really wanted.

Once Sam fully owned his unique relationship ideals and could see how honesty and transparency created safety, he started becoming truthful in his interactions with women. Today, he's upfront about what he's looking for in a relationship, which creates a high level of safety for himself and anyone he dates. Sam doesn't deny wanting to have sex, and he keeps his agreements with the women he dates, and everyone knows where they stand. Only with this level of honesty could the perfect match for him show up. Today, Sam has a thriving sex life, and he has a special sweetie who he's fallen in love with.

The impulse to protect and deny can take priority over taking responsibility for the impact our actions have on other people. While blaming the victim is never okay, survivors of sexual abuse also have a responsibility to heal themselves so they can have access to their voices and don't unintentionally set themselves up to be re-victimized. When someone hasn't healed themselves of past trauma, they can feel victimized in situations where they should have or could have taken responsibility for their personal space, which is what happened with the woman who accused Sam of violating her.

The best way to keep yourself sexually safe is to fully heal yourself. When you're healed, you'll know what your boundaries are and will be able to speak up. You'll also only choose to be in relationship with people who honor your boundaries.

Today, as a survivor of sexual abuse who has chosen to heal, I can now stop someone from getting too close to me in unhealthy ways which is completely different from the freeze trauma response I shared earlier about the man who approached me in the pool. I didn't have the capacity to stop someone I had never met before from getting close enough to put his arm around me.

This is where the ability to hold conflicting ideas at the same time is essential.

- I didn't do anything wrong.

And...

- I didn't stop him from getting closer than I was comfortable with.

Just as survivors of sexual abuse need to hold two ideas at the same time to heal, so do sexual offenders, so their protective mechanisms can soften, and they can look at their own behavior from a more objective perspective. Everyone is safer when we each take responsibility for our sexuality and heal our early wounding. One of the consequences of denying our sexuality is that the potential to hurt other people increases.

Only when Sam felt held in love could he acknowledge how not keeping agreements could harm another person. Only when he was listened to could he see how arbitrarily changing an agreement with someone who was vulnerable would leave them feeling unsafe and would also leave him vulnerable to being accused of rape.

Sam made amends and a commitment: to be honest and forthcoming with his intentions and to keep his agreements even in the face of heightened desire.

> *Golden Repair, Kintsukuroi: The Japanese art of treating breakage and repair as part of the history of an object, rather than something to disguise.*

While we're not our wounds, they're part of our life experience which needs integration. Punishing ourselves won't free us from the past or stop abuse from happening in the future. Shaming ourselves keeps the pain stuck whereas telling the truth leads to freedom. We need a kind and compassionate way to relate to ourselves and the people who hurt us. And we need to bring awareness to what needs healing.

Gap Work: What Still Needs Healing?

You're already stuck with yourself for a lifetime.
Why not improve this relationship?
~Vironika Tugaleva

Get out your journal and set aside at least thirty minutes. Give yourself tenderness for the wounded parts that need healing as you answer these questions:

1. The parts of me that have been most hurt are...
2. What I've been telling myself that is most hurtful is...
3. The healing I most need is...
4. If I were completely healed from the past, I would...
5. The kindness I need is...

Now that you've identified the parts of you that most need healing, extend love and compassion to yourself as you acknowledge everything you've just written. Hold yourself in love and simply acknowledge each thing you wrote. All of what you wrote needs your love.

For example, if you said that your innocent heart is a part that has been most hurt, then say something like this: "Sweetheart, I see your innocent heart has been hurt." Then take a breath.

Repeat this step for each answer you gave.

When you are complete, simply sit in sacred silence for a few moments. You might want to do something nourishing for yourself after this exercise, like taking a walk or giving yourself a relaxing bath.

Retributive vs. Restorative Justice

We but mirror the world. All the tendencies present in the outer world are to be found in the world of our body. If we could change ourselves, the tendencies in the world would also change. As a man changes his own nature, so does the attitude of the world change toward him.
~Mahatma Gandhi

Sexual abuse is a sensitive topic that holds a lot of emotion for many of us. History reveals sexual offenders can expect to lose everything they care about including their family, their livelihood, and status in their community and world. When a person does take responsibility, they're treated like a villain. Even the threat of prison discourages sexual offenders from taking responsibility or seeking help to stop their behavior.

Ironically, if the offender doesn't take responsibility, the survivors of abuse can end up re-living the abuse if they're asked to testify in court, even when they've worked through their trauma.

There's simply too much at stake for the typical offender to take any kind of responsibility. We can see this happening with public figures and at the highest level of our justice system with the confirmation of Supreme Court Justice Kavanaugh. When we have a society that makes it possible for the offender to admit what they've done without losing everything, then we'll have a culture of responsibility instead of a culture of victimization.

Restorative Justice

> Restorative Justice is part of the criminal justice system that focuses on repairing the harm done and includes not only direct victims, but everyone impacted by the crime. Restorative justice is a powerful and

valued process revered in prisons with long waiting lists for participation.[13]

This section is particularly relevant for those who want to understand how restorative justice works and are considering engaging in a restorative process instead of a retributive one.

Our current justice model punishes behavior but doesn't reveal the source of behavior or address how to heal the person who harms others. Retributive justice theory calls for the offender to suffer. Its roots are found in the Torah, Mosaic Law from the Old Testament, and in the Code of Hammurabi, a legal text from the 1700s. All call for punishing someone for what they've done. The well-known biblical scripture our social justice system tends to follow is "An eye for an eye."

> *An eye for an eye makes the whole world blind.*
> *~Mahatma Gandhi*

In contrast, restorative justice theory prioritizes repairing the harm done and addresses the underlying reasons the crime was committed. Through deep and thoughtful contemplation, those who caused harm are guided through a restorative process to discover what led them to cause harm. They include the person they harmed, the families of the victim, their friends and family, themselves, and the community at large.

Restorative justice is an approach which supports the journey back to wholeness for everyone impacted by the harm done and includes the people who have done harm in the solution instead of treating them like a problem to get rid of. As I mentioned already, my advocacy for a restorative model is for the regressed sexual offender. "D. Richard Laws states that rather than treating [regressed sexual] offenders as risk-laden deviants, they should be treated as fellow human beings who can achieve more productive lives with proper guidance (Franklin, K, 2011)."[14] I imagine Justice Ketanji Brown Jackson was using a restorative justice model when making her controversial sentencing choices around sexual offenders which were brought to light during her historic Supreme Court confirmation hearing.

---

[13] http://restorativejustice.org/#sthash.ctE2wziC.dpbs
[14] http://sexual-offender-treatment.org/101.html

Abuse is never okay. Ever. If the fear of punishment worked to deter childhood sexual abuse, then it would have ended a long time ago. Our current model just isn't working, and a restorative model could be the answer. A restorative model would lead to the offender offering a valuable perspective into what leads to abusive behavior so we can learn what caused them to hurt someone and how to stop abuse before it happens.

I can attest to the power and level of personal accountability taken by people who engage in a restorative justice process. Working inside a California state prison, I became aware of how hurt people hurt people and was privileged to witness how the healing of one person has the potential to heal everyone harmed. I'm inspired by the courage of those who have caused harm and are willing to be honest and share the true details of the crime they committed and take full responsibility in the service of healing and repair for everyone involved.

Restorative practices are certainly not for everyone, but they worked for me and my family. Under certain circumstances, they can work for you too. The abused and abuser are part of the same social fabric we all live in. We can't afford to see ourselves as separate from crime or the people who commit crimes. Treating the offender as inhuman, we miss valuable opportunities to find solutions to the underlying reasons people cause harm.

We need to have intelligent open conversations exploring early childhood interventions with an emphasis on investing in the lives of children and their parents *before* abuse ever happens.

Preparing to Have Difficult Conversations

> *The character of a man is known by his conversations.*
> *~Menander*

When I worked with the Insight Prison Project, I facilitated an eighteen-month Victim Offender Education Group (VOEG) to prepare incarcerated people and victims of crimes to sit in a circle together and have a healing conversation. The purpose of VOEG is to help incarcerated people gain insight into what led them to prison and take responsibility for the impact of their choices. Unresolved early childhood trauma was an experience that *every* participant of the program shared.

One teaching of the VOEG curriculum was to guide participants to share their experience using the language of accountability. Participation in the program is conditional on a person's willingness and ability to take responsibility for the harm they caused. I witnessed healing at the deepest level when each person took responsibility during these difficult conversations. Incarcerated women transformed before me. They experienced a freedom typically not possible while incarcerated.

We're all imprisoned until we take responsibility for our choices. People who caused harm are responsible for the impact of what they did, but people who are harmed are also responsible for what they do *after* they've been harmed. It worked for me to confront my father directly because I felt safe. If you want to address the person who caused you harm, please get support to prepare you for a conversation and to create safety for yourself.

Here are some recommendations to get started:

- Work with a therapist or coach who has experience with survivors of childhood sexual abuse and who also specializes in mediating difficult conversations.
- Take as much time as you need to know what you want to communicate and the results you want through having the conversation.
- Create a plan for ongoing support after the conversation so you can integrate your experience.

Part Seven
Living Beyond The Gap

A kind of light spread out from her. And everything changed color. And the world opened out. And a day was good to awaken to. And there were no limits to anything. And the people of the world were good and handsome.
And I was not afraid any more.
~ John Steinbeck, East of Eden

Transformation requires creating new habitual ways of being, which takes time. You can know everything at an intellectual level yet have nothing change in your life. To truly get freedom from shame, you'll need to integrate everything you're learning here into your daily life. The exercises you've completed in this book are meant to be revisited. Use the tools given to strengthen your foundation. Here are some keys to remember as you continue your journey toward wholeness:

- Choose your perspectives consciously. Remember, the meaning you make about what happened creates the lens you live your life through.
- Take responsibility for yourself and your healing to increase your capacity to create happy healthy relationships.
- Consistently take new actions until they become the new way of being.
- Deepen your ability to stay present no matter what's happening in your life.
- Practice being authentic with yourself and others.
- Take risks by telling the truth even when you're afraid.
- Be honest about your feelings and needs.
- Stay aware of what triggers you into old patterns.

Beyond The Gap: My Wound is My Gift

That is all I want in life: for this pain to seem purposeful.
~Elizabeth Wurtzel, Prozac Nation

You can heal and still the impact of the abuse will continue to affect you in various degrees throughout your life. Being able to accurately name the abuse and its impact without judgment leads to freedom. It takes practice and repetition to grow self-compassion and to be soft and gentle with yourself when naming the effects abuse has had. Now that you've made a fair amount of discovery, it's time to claim some of the gifts from what happened to you.

While abuse can leave a devastating impact on your life, you aren't doomed to be negatively impacted by what happened. You're *not* your experience, but who you are includes your experience. Integrating the experience of sexual abuse is a lifelong journey which continues to allow for more authentic relatedness, more healthy living, and more possibilities for meaningful contribution.

Life's greatest wounds bring wisdom and compassion that can bring healing to many people. You can turn your wound into a contribution, that makes a difference in the world. You don't have to deny what happened to you to create safety for yourself. You don't have to pretend what happened didn't happen to thrive in your life. And you don't have to unconsciously react to what happened in the past. It may be a rough journey through the pain, but joy and freedom are on the other side as false beliefs fall away and you remember the truth of who you really are. As you reconnect with your sacredness, your life will start to unfold in beautiful ways.

I've changed from being hurt and angry about what happened to me to being grateful for every heartache I've experienced. Through decades of self-abandonment, I lived my life feeling disconnected from others, but as I've learned how to stay with myself, I feel connected to all of life. When I was living with debilitating shame, I unconsciously hurt myself. When I *believed* I didn't matter, I unconsciously hurt the people I love the most leaving them to believe they don't matter to me. When I'm connected to the truth without inflating or deflating how much I matter, then I take care of what matters most to me including the people in my life and the contribution I want to make.

While the residue of having been hurt can affect every aspect of your life, everything changes when you relate to what happened to you as part of a spiritual journey guiding you back to your inherent wholeness. As I've integrated my experience of abuse, I've come to know that I'm not the abuse. I feel inspired to make the pain and shame I lived through worth it by helping others. I've become a person who can hold the deepest darkest parts of another's deeply personal experience of shame and self-criticism without judgment or harshness because I'm able to hold my own experience with compassion.

You may not be able to see the gold in your experience right now, but knowing gifts come from the worst of circumstances can support you to keep moving forward. Continue on this worthwhile journey and you'll discover wisdom and gifts to offer the world. It's the price you've paid; make it worth it!

The corner of a tiny blue tarp sticking out of the sand on a beach in Thailand helped me see sexual abuse in a deeply personal way, and it also gave me a global perspective that still guides me today.

> Warm white sands and mature healthy trees lined the entire coastline of a small, deserted island beach in Thailand. Our small group got off the longtail boat to get closer to the beauty but made a devastating discovery. We walked barefoot into the tree line and stepped right into a literal garbage dump of hidden washed-up trash entangled in the branches and roots of thousands of trees and brush. I stared in disbelief and felt the same crushing despair I had felt when I was sexually abused by my father decades earlier.
>
> How could something so beautiful be so deeply damaged? "Who did this?" I asked under my breath feeling victimized by the sheer volume of plastic bottles and food wrappers, many of which I recognized from where I lived in the United States.
>
> Then we got to work.
>
> We each took a few extra-large trash bags and scampered off in different directions to save the world. While my friends energetically filled their bags with a variety of litter, I sat under a tree grasping a two-inch piece of blue plastic protruding from the wet sand.

I pulled, but it didn't move. In frustration, I pulled harder, and the earth held even tighter. Then a wave washed over the small triangle I was holding between my fingers and a tiny bit more blue plastic peeked back at me. I fell into a rhythm, a sort of meditation as my body moved with the sand and waves in what felt like an intimate dance with life. The earth and I were lovers in deep union. With the sand between my toes and the saltwater caressing my feet, we were talking to each other in our own sacred language.

The waves attuned to the rhythm of my breath and with each crash of water Mother Earth relinquished a little more of her grip. I reassured her, and hours later when the fifteen-foot square tarp had been fully released, I sat and cried salty tears with her.

I learned that Mother Earth takes everything we give her. No matter what's thrown at her, she keeps giving something beautiful back. For all the harm inflicted on her, she just keeps giving back beauty. When I take the time to be with her, on her terms, then she freely gives me what I need. She is whole and complete and doesn't take anything personally.

That's who I want to be.

I went home with a new sense of responsibility to create something beautiful out of what happened to me when I was a kid. For many years after the abuse ended, I felt like the devastated shoreline. But unlike the earth, I felt victimized by what happened to me and didn't know how to use what was thrown my way for good. Mother Earth taught me well, and I'll never forget that beach in Thailand where I discovered that healing happens from the inside out and *everything* can be transformed.

I returned home with a longing to create something beautiful out of what happened to me. I didn't know how at the time, but here I am. I've contemplated this sacred experience in Thailand for many years, and today, here on these pages, I'm turning my difficult past into a loving gift that others can benefit from. To honor the sacredness of life, I've turned the raw material of abuse into fertile soil and created a beautiful and fulfilling life of joy and authenticity.

If I can turn what happened to me into a gift, so can you.

> *The wholeness and freedom we seek is our true nature, who we really are.*
> *~Jack Kornfield*

Now it's your turn to discover something positive from the unspeakable.

Gap Work: Your Wound Is Your Gift

> *Where your wound lies, so lies your greatest gifts.*
> *~Joseph Campbell*

To claim your gifts, you need to understand that what you went through in childhood helped make you who you are today. In reading this book and doing the exercises, you're aware of so much more about yourself and the impact of your past. As you continue to integrate your early wounding, you'll become more of your authentic self and increase your capacity to create a healthy life.

Get out your journal and let's take a step toward revealing your gifts.

To claim your gifts, you don't need to have all the answers today. You only need to be willing to recognize the ways you've grown, developed, and evolved because of your early childhood wounding.

Answer these questions to get connected to your gifts.

- What are the qualities that I most care about and want to develop? (Review the list of positive qualities and name them here.)
- How do I most want to express the qualities I just named?
- What do I most want to change about the world?
- Who do I most want to help?
- If I had a message to give the people of the world, what would I want them to know?
- In what ways do I most want to impact the world for good?

Now that you have taken some time to get connected to what you care about, take about fifteen minutes to journal what you're aware of after answering the above questions.

After you've journaled, ask yourself these questions:

- Is there a line of work I'm drawn to, or people I want to help?
- Are there skills I would like to develop so I can help others?
- Is there a training I've been wanting to take but haven't been able to?

You don't need to know how to turn what you've been through into a gift; you only need to know that you can. Let's identify one small or big action you can take to move yourself forward, such as:

- Going back to school.
- Hiring a therapist.
- Volunteering.

Sexuality: Reclaiming All of Yourself

There are two mistakes one can make along the road to truth... not going all the way, and not starting.
~Siddhartha Gautama

I stopped the abuse from continuing by saying no. The abuse ended, but so did the connection I wanted. In my young mind, I made up the belief that saying no makes people go away. Instead of understanding the power I had to stop abuse, I grew up believing if I said no, then I would be alone.

I believed having my own opinions or taking a stand for myself would alienate people and I would be left alone and unloved, so I disappeared myself and became a chameleon in my intimate relationships. I used my sexuality to fill my need for connection. I wasn't aware the fear of abandonment was running my life.

Reclaiming yourself is a process of returning to wholeness and includes the following:

- A return to innocence.
- Embodying personal power.
- Reclaiming sexuality.

Returning to wholeness includes having an understanding of what healthy sexuality is.

Healthy Sexuality

Sexual education in our society is weak at best and politicized at worst. Most people don't have a healthy relationship with their own sexuality and are inadequate at teaching healthy sexuality to their children. In general, parents and caregivers either feel relief the schools are teaching what they're uncomfortable talking about or they protest sex education being taught in schools altogether. Children shouldn't be expected to know what's okay without being explicitly taught. Even if their parents had "The Talk," rarely do people share a positive experience of learning about their body and what healthy sexuality is growing up.

Human sexuality is much more complex than a sexual act. Society is left with a distorted, incomplete, and insufficient understanding of what's normal and healthy around sex and sexuality. The foundation of healthy sexuality includes being able to equally say yes or no to sex, to freely share your feelings and values about sex, and to enjoy your sexual expression without shame.

Where do you go to find answers? How do you access accurate information when what's true has been withheld, hidden, or distorted? Believing what you've made up in your mind from an early abusive experience makes it difficult to create a healthy relationship with your body and your sexuality. Adults cannot be expected to feel comfortable talking about sexuality with their children when nobody discussed what is healthy and normal sexuality when they were kids.

With the exception of medical procedures, such as invitro fertilization, everyone is conceived through a sexual act. Sexual acts can be loving interactions between two consenting adults or the result of a violation of an abuse of power such as rape or incest. When non-consensual sex happens, a future healthy relationship with sexuality gets even more convoluted and difficult to experience. Now, let's take a look at healthy sexuality in adults.

Sexually Healthy Adults

> *Our sexuality affects everything we do, and everything affects our sexuality. The same is true of our spirituality—that which is most deeply meaningful to us. We can deny both. But denying them does not mean they are not both alive in every breath and heartbeat of life.*
> ~Tina Schermer Sellers, Sex, God, and the Conservative Church

While there's so much to learn, it's possible to reconnect with your innocence and find healthy ways to express your sexuality starting today. On the next two pages are some characteristics of sexually healthy adults shown in a chart created by Hadsall and Associates.[15]

---

[15] https://www.health.state.mn.us/people/sexualhealth/characteristics.pdf created by Hadsall and Associates 2001, revised 2010, reproduced for ease of reading

CHARACTERISTICS OF SEXUALLY HEALTHY ADULTS

From a holistic perspective, sexual health includes emotional, psychological, physical, intellectual and spiritual dimensions. The following are characteristics of sexually healthy adults however sexual health is developed over a lifespan from cradle to grave. Integrating sexuality into one's life in a balanced way is a life-time endeavor.

Communication

- Interact with all genders in appropriate and respectful ways
- Communicate effectively with family and friends
- Ask questions of other adults about sexual issues, when necessary
- Are able to communicate and negotiate sexual limits
- Communicate respectfully their desires to have sex and not to have sex
- Accept refusals of sex without hostility or feeling insulted
- Can physically express feelings of attraction and desire in ways that do not focus on the genitals (ex: holding, caressing, kissing, etc.)
- Talk with a partner about sexual activity before it occurs, including limits, contraceptive and condom use, and meaning in the relationship
- Communicate with partners their intentions for the relationships (ex: only dating, want marriage)
- Listen to and respect others' boundaries and limits
- Are sensitive to non-verbal cues of others' boundaries and limits

Relationships

- Develop friendships that do not have a sexual agenda
- Avoid exploitative relationships
- Choose partners who are responsible, trustworthy, safe and giving
- Can be sexually intimate without being physical (ex: talk about sexual feelings, verbally express attraction, do things that awaken desire in partner)
- Can express themselves in ways other than genitally (ex: holding, caressing, kissing, etc.)
- Take personal responsibility for their own boundaries

Self-esteem, Self-worth

- Appreciate their own bodies
- Are sensually aware and able to stay conscious in their bodies
- Can touch their own bodies without feeling shame or disgust
- Allow themselves to experience pleasurable sensual and sexual feelings
- Have the capacity to nurture themselves and others, and accept nurturing from others
- Feel joy in sexual experiences of their choosing
- Know when they need touch rather than sex and try to get their needs for touch met appropriately
- Have developed sense of self, an understanding of who they are
- Enjoy sexual feelings without necessarily acting upon them
- Accept refusals of sex without hostility or feeling personally insulted
- Allow themselves to be vulnerable
- Are comfortable with their sexual identity and orientation
- Are becoming aware of the impact of negative sexual experiences such as sexual abuse, and the impact of negative cultural messages on their sexual development
- Are taking steps to address issues that have arisen as a result of past experiences
- Feel confident in their ability to set appropriate boundaries
- Realized that, by working through sexual issues, individuals may heal psychological and emotional wounding from past experiences and damaging beliefs

CHARACTERISTICS OF SEXUALLY HEALTHY ADULTS	
Education • Realize the consequences of sexual activity • Comprehend the impact of media messages on thoughts, feelings, values, and behaviors related to sexuality • Understand that the drive for sex is powerful and can be integrated into one's life in positive and healthy ways • Respect the right of all people to enjoy and engage in the full range of consensual, nonexploitive sexual behaviors	**Contraception, protection, body integrity** • Take responsibility for their own bodies and their own orgasms • If sexually active, use contraception effectively to avoid pregnancy and use condoms and safer sex to avoid contracting or spreading a sexually transmitted disease • Practice health-promoting behaviors, such as regular checkups, breast or testicular self-exams, regular and routine testing for STDs
Values • Decide on what is personally "right" and act on these values • Demonstrate tolerance for people with different values • Are not threatened by others with sexual orientation different from theirs • Show respect to others whose cultural values, ethnic heritage, age, socio-economic status, religion, and gender are different from theirs	**Spirituality** • Honor the sacred aspect of sexual union • Understand that sexual energy is not separate from being human • Understand that sexual union is one way human beings connect body and soul

Healthy sexuality can feel elusive for survivors of sexual abuse. Nobody taught me how to have a healthy relationship with my sexuality. In my early adulthood, I experienced my sexuality through confusing flashbacks and memories of the abuse. Because I didn't understand what was happening to me, I believed there was something wrong with me. The communication between my husband and me was tenuous at best because I had never been taught how to talk about what I was feeling.

Having to figure my healing out all by myself deepened my confusion and brought more shame. The shaming question I asked myself was, "Why is this happening to me?" I discovered better questions like, "What do I need to feel cherished?"

I started challenging my beliefs around sex and my relationship to my sexuality in my early forties. I participated in a series of workshops on sex, love, and intimacy with the Human Awareness Institute which advocates for a world where people live in dignity, respect, understanding, trust, kindness, compassion, reverence, honesty, and love, a fabulous vision that all of humanity would benefit from.

I arrived at my first gender-balanced workshop with a low-grade terror I kept hidden just under my radar. One deeply rooted belief I held before the workshop was that the only thing men want is sex. Joe was a handsome charismatic man who arrived the same time I did—and he confirmed my greatest fear while walking to the registration table together.

"What brought you to this workshop?" I asked.

He said he was attending the workshop because he heard it would be easy for him to find someone to have sex with. My inauthentic smile hid the discomfort I felt inside. I deepened my conviction that my beliefs were true and when we ended up assigned to sleep next to each other in the dormitory, I convinced myself I was a goner. I wouldn't have known how to say no if he wanted to have sex with me. Lucky for me he didn't try, but later in the workshop I was sure he wanted to.

The program began with the facilitator teaching a model for communicating with each other in ways not many people are used to. Our first topic of conversation focused around sharing our sexual histories, which is something I had never done before at that level—even with my husband.

Each exercise the facilitators guided us through became increasingly difficult as the weekend progressed. I met my limit and couldn't continue when I was paired with Joe in a small group exercise. I reached out to the facilitator who met with us to help me communicate to the group in a deeply authentic way. Trembling, I shared the beliefs which fed my fears to the members of my group.

Then the unexpected happened.

Joe shared how deeply my vulnerability impacted him. His reverence for me was palpable. For the first time in my life, I felt my body (and my entire being) was being honored and respected. Through taking the risk to bring all of myself forward, I learned I can create safety for myself by showing up fully in relationship with others.

Reflecting on what Joe modeled for me, I learned two important lessons.

The first lesson is most men do want sex, but that's not all they want. Most men want realness, vulnerability, connection, closeness, and authenticity. And sex.

> The second lesson I learned was how safety can be created when someone owns their sexuality. Joe could clearly state what he wanted and didn't want, which is something I couldn't do until after the workshop. We completed the exercise with mutual respect intact and I left the workshop with a new friend who I didn't have to worry about having sex with—unless I wanted to.

After the workshop I could see how growing up in a sex-positive culture could contribute to ending sexual abuse. Developing healthy sexuality after having been abused takes effort, commitment, and time. I continued to learn more about myself and how to relate to my sexual self in healthy ways. Eventually, I stopped having flashbacks of the abuse and satisfying sexual experiences with my partner became the norm.

Gap Work: Healthy Sexuality

> *As my world expands so do my heart and mind. I am willing to stay open and accept all the miracles and abundance the universe has to offer me.*
> *~Kris Carr*

Creating a healthy relationship with your sexuality starts with giving yourself permission to be right where you are. Get out your journal. Take time to contemplate what's most important to you when choosing a partner.

- What does intimacy mean to me?
- What typically happens in my sexual relationships?
- What do I need to have a presence of to feel safe in a sexual relationship?
- What do I find most difficult to discuss with a potential partner?
- What do I do to create safety in my sexual relationships?
- What do I do to create a lack of safety in my sexual relationships?

On a scale of one to five, with one being the least true and five being the truest, rate the following statements:

- I know what I want in a sexual relationship.
- Before having a new sexual partner, I consider if the person is a good choice for me.

- Before having a new sexual partner, I consider if the timing is right for me.
- I have a safe sex conversation before having sex with a new partner.
- I make it a priority to share important information, like sexually transmitted diseases, including when I was last tested.
- I discuss birth control options before having sex.
- I communicate what I want clearly to my potential partner(s) before becoming sexual with them.

Now take about thirty minutes to answer the following questions:

- What heartbreak do you have around your sexuality?
- What would you most like your relationship with your sexuality to look like?
- What would bring healing to your relationship with your sexuality?

Keeping Children Safe: Children's Sexual Behaviors

Don't turn your face away.
Once you've seen, you can no longer act like you don't know.
Open your eyes to the truth. It's all around you.
Don't deny what the eyes to your soul have revealed to you.

Now that you know, you cannot feign ignorance.
Now that you're aware of the problem, you cannot pretend you don't care.
To be concerned is to be human.
To act is to care.
~Vashti Quiroz-Vega[16]

Research has shown that up to 85 percent of children's sexual behavior is natural and healthy. If you've been sexually abused, you could be unnecessarily concerned about sexual behavior you witness in your children or you could ignore behavior which needs addressing.

Take time to educate yourself on which sexual behaviors are developmentally appropriate so you don't turn your children's normal behavior into the darkness of shame. Educate yourself on which behaviors are problematic so you know what to pay attention to and don't miss any red flags that indicate abuse is happening.

Toni Cavanagh Johnson, PhD wrote an informative forty-two-page booklet called, *Understanding Children's Sexual Behaviors: What's Natural and Healthy*.

Toni Cavanagh Johnson helps parents and caregivers:

---

[16] Quiroz-Vega, Vashti from *The Writer Next Door.* Found on Good Reads and reprinted with permission from author.

- Identify healthy and worrisome behaviors in children.
- Understand how to engage with children when you identify healthy behaviors.
- Know when to intervene when you identify worrisome behaviors.
- Know when to seek professional help.

When you have the tools, you can guide your children toward healthy sexuality. Learn how to talk to your children when they ask questions and how to respond to their normal and concerning sexual behavior in ways that are helpful instead of harmful.

Natural and healthy behavior changes as children grow and develop. Here's an example of what Toni Cavanaugh describes as natural behavior, concerning behavior, and behavior that needs you to seek professional help for fourth grade children.

- **Natural** and healthy behavior when fourth graders ask about genitals and where babies come from.
- **Concerning** behavior when fourth graders show fear and anxiety about sexual topics instead of curiosity.
- **Seek professional help** when fourth graders ask endless questions after curiosity has been satisfied and/or have sexual knowledge too advanced for their age.

Epilogue

> *Your task is not to seek for love, but merely to seek and find all the barriers within yourself that you've built against it.*
> ~Rumi

My father died while I was writing this book. I'd like you to know the human being I knew and grew to deeply admire and respect. My father wasn't perfect, but he was a man who grew to be perfect in love. He contributed to his friends and his family with his courage and presence. My father was a self-made man of substance, integrity, depth, and generosity.

My story isn't about the harm my father caused, it's about the good he created and the contribution he made to ending sexual abuse in our family.

There's no time for grievances.

While you may not know how to take your life back from the past, here's what needs to happen:

- Forgive for your own sake.
- Do what makes you happy and brings you joy.
- Live authentically.
- Stop believing there is anything wrong with you.
- Align with your future—fake it till you make it.
- Don't take anything personally.
- What someone thinks about you is none of your business.
- Give yourself permission to make new choices.
- Get help when you need it.
- And most importantly, Let go of shame—it only keeps you stuck in the past.

Together, and separately, my father and I made our vision for a safe family a reality. While my story reveals the potential benefits from forgiveness and inclusion, it's more personally relevant to know the power and possibilities for yourself when you get out of victimization and take full responsibility for the life you choose to create. Now I'm inviting you to make your life what you want it to be. The effort you put into healing your heart will be worth it. Align all of yourself with the future you long for. Align all your thinking and beliefs with the intention you set at the beginning of this book.

My intention is that sharing my journey with you in the way I have helps you remember your inherent wholeness, honor the sacredness of your precious life, and live your full authentic expression of love. May you find peace and enduring happiness in the present regardless of what you experienced as a child.

Acknowledgments

> *"I'm a success today because I had a friend who believed in me and I didn't have the heart to let him down."*
> *~Abraham Lincoln*

I've heard you never get to success by yourself. I certainly haven't. I've had countless people loving me, inviting me to stand on their shoulders, holding my hand out to lift me up. Thank you to all those who held me up when I didn't know how to do it myself. This book wouldn't be here it if weren't for you.

Thank you to Michelle Vandepas, for teaching me how to live with an open heart, for believing in and contributing to this book by giving me an entire team at GracePoint Publishing. To my first editor Christina Dreve, for endlessly encouraging me to keep going and giving me permission to write my first "shitty" draft. Thank you for your loving support, direct feedback, and expert guidance and for holding my feet to the fire. To Laurie, Carly, and Lexi, you're miracle workers. And to Tascha Yoder, I don't even have words; thank you for wading in the weeds with me until the very end. I AM so supported.

Thank you to Marci Shimoff, for your generosity of spirit; for opening the doors to your heart, to your home, and to my future. Thank you for encouraging me to get my graduate degree, I have my MSW because of you. Thank you for holding me in love when I experienced deep loss and disappointment. Thank you for trusting me with thousands of your clients' hearts and for celebrating my hard-earned success. I still hear the tinkling of the bell you rang for me on so many occasions. You're the real deal, my dear friend—inside and out!

Thank you to Katherine Woodward Thomas, for *insisting* I write this book and holding me close when I floundered. Thank you for shining your light on me and gently pushing me until my light could stand on its own. Thank you for saying yes to God and creating a body of work this world needs; your teaching lives in and through me. My dear, brilliant friend, I pray that you know the depth of your contribution to me and to my life. Thank you for giving me my leaders-of-love sisters. To Paula, Wendy, Jana, Joan, and Michele, I am forever grateful for the ways you hold me in who I'm becoming instead of who I've been, and that's an ever-expanding journey.

Thank you to Leonard Szymczak, for your generosity for mentoring me in all of what's involved in becoming an author—I honestly had no idea. To my "last stretch" reading team friends, Charmaine Cusick, Kelly Mcguigan, Rachel Puryear, Heatherly Stanky, Julie Stamper, and Grady Fort, thank you for the endless time you invested in giving constructive and valuable feedback. I'm blown away by your generosity and willingness to support me so fully.

Thank you to the many teachers I've had and the trainings I've been privileged to participate in: To my dear spiritual teacher and guide, Jennifer Welwood, thank you for bringing all of yourself to the path of awakening and pointing me in the direction of mine. I've had glimpses because of you. And to my Sangha family, thank you for your transparency and vulnerability in showing up with me on and off the cushion. Thank you, I love you.

To Debbie Ford, for shining a light on my shadows in a way I could tolerate seeing them. To Shauna Wilson and Gordon Clay, for supporting my father and I in healing beyond what I thought possible. To my Hakomi teachers Scott Eaton, Manuela Mischke-Reeds, and Shai Lavie, for your loving guidance and presence and helping me to enjoy staying in my body. To Roma Cardenas and Mrs. Olsen, for being a light during deep suffering. To the wonderful therapists I've had including Marsha Nohl and Jackie Danielson, thank you for your generosity and wise counsel—and especially for loving me unconditionally. I needed that.

Thank you to all the amazing clients, who I also consider as friends and have had the privilege of working with over the past two decades. Thank you for trusting me and letting me contribute to your life. I've grown tremendously through witnessing your courage and commitment to break free from the past. I'm inspired by your willingness to take the risk to live authentically and I live in awe of your beautiful human beingness. You've impacted every page I've written.

Thank you to all the fabulous people who served me in restaurants and café's while I wrote this book. Especially my Starbucks crew Lisa, Alexia, Lily, Bean, Joseline, and Dariana, thank you for taking really good care of me for hours (and years) on end. Your kindness matters.

To my Hakomi practice buddies Karen Daley, Allison Bryant, and Grady Fort, thank you for letting me fall apart, for letting me practice on you when I don't know what I'm doing, and for making me a better practitioner and a better person.

To the leaders of restorative justice programs around the world, thank you for the work you do in creating a pathway for repair. Thank you to those who trained me, especially Rochelle Edwards who created a restorative curriculum and gave me the opportunity to contribute. Thank you to my dear co-facilitators who were inside Chowchilla and are now free, Carde Taylor and Michele Scott, you inspire me every day to live free from limitation. Thank you to *all* the courageous women in our groups who laid their broken hearts on the table for everyone to hold in love. Your vulnerability and courage have impacted me more than you'll ever know. Thank you. I love you.

Thank you to my wonderful friends. To Shelley Griswold, for all the sacrifices you've made to take care of me. To Deb Leoni, for laser coaching and laughing through the hardest times when we should be crying instead. To Meta Mehling, for making me a priority in your life and always showing me how much you care, and for forgiving me when I fall short. To Gerise Pappas, for seeing into my soul and then letting me see myself through your eyes. To Catherine Young, for getting me through one of the darkest times of my life without even knowing you did that. To Doug Kaplan, for the wonderful breakfast talks and warm friendship. To WD for being my first confidant and Carmine Morreale—thank you both being some of my strongest ties to my father and family. To Yvonne "Cookie" Rios for *always* praying for me and reminding me what matters most. To Debbie Moore-Yip, for decades of easy sisterhood. To Paula Whitely, for jumping in and helping when my father was dying and for holding such a big perspective. To Robert Schmid, for all the impromptu dinners and chuckles. To my Tribe Evolve Family, Rachel, Kwame, Heatherly, Mike, Chris, Hala, Shawn, Lisa, and Markus, thank you for your celebratory energy and breathing life into this crazy world. To Aaron Hodges, for the respite you are in my life. To Dan Carrigan, for listening without judgment and letting me be imperfect. To Al Chan, for your infectious zest for adventure and taking me to the ballpark, even if it is only once a year. To Jerry Bowes, for bringing your manliness to my home to trim trees and have deep meaningful talks. To Josh Cohen, for the doors you opened. And to some of my newer friends, Catalina Payne, Kimberly O'Hara, Debbi Daschinger, and Bill Aviles, thank you for being true to your dreams and inspiring me to stay to true to mine. To all my friends, mentioned or not, thank you for playing and working with me. Thank you for laughing and crying with me. Thank you for pushing me and letting me dig my heels in. You're all treasures in my life.

Thank you to everyone who showed up during my father's transition and for holding us both in love, especially Nic Colyer, Scotty Lewis, and Richard Schieffer, for keeping watch with me and taking care of me while I tended to my father. Thank you to the mighty men in my father's "I" group for inviting me to be an honorary member when you released him from service.

Thank you to my family. To my brother Danny, for being a steadfast support and anchor in my life. To my sister-in-law Ana, for sharing your lightness of being and joyful spirit, which we all need. To my sister Tammie and my sister-in-law Chello, for the belly laughs that nobody else would understand. To my niece, Lexi and my grandniece, Charlie, for the precious time we shared. To my nephew Austin, for receiving the gift from your grandpa. To Jesse and Kristin, for accepting me and including me as your family. To my niece, Lily, for being the legacy that brings us all together. To the rest of my family near and wide, especially, Courtnie Reyes for giving me Apollo and Alia, and to Brenda Peabody for giving me Jeramiah and Bailey. And to my cousin Jaleen for our late-night talks, thank you, thank you, thank you. I love you all dearly.

To my parents: To my mother, Terrie, my deepest regret is not gaining freedom from my pain until it was too late to love you the way I now know how to love. Thank you for saying yes on the last day of your life so I could hold you in my arms as you left this world. To my mom, Katie, thank you for the depth of your convictions and for holding me, my father, and our entire combined family in love. To my father, Rust, thank you for being brave in facing your demons and giving me the only gift I ever needed—a safe father for myself, a safe grandfather for my kids, and a life purpose to end the impact of sexual abuse on our broken hearts.

And most of all, thank you to my greatest teachers, my kids, Sergio and Aviana, for forgiving my imperfections, especially when I should have known better. Thank you for being patient with me over the years as I continue to learn and grow. I hope to be a mother and friend you can be proud of. And to my grandkids, my newest reason for wanting to create a world where children are nurtured, cared for, and cherished.

Writing this acknowledgement, I'm realizing with deep gratitude, and awareness that I've never been alone, and I've always been held in love. I hope you all know how much I love you.

References

Anonymous. "Has Our Culture Really Changed?" https://english.cofc.edu/first-year-writing/Has Our Culture Really Changed.pdf

Anonymous. "The History of Rape Culture" http://historyofrapeculture.weebly.com/contemporary-rape-culturepopular-culture.html

Anonymous. Wikipedia Four stages of competence https://en.wikipedia.org/wiki/Four_stages_of_competence

Douglas, A., Stolz-Newton, M., Grant, Natalie S. "The use of yoga to build self-compassion as a healing method for survivors of sexual violence." https://self-compassion.org/wp-content/uploads/2017/01/Crews2016.pdf

Gabaya, R., Hameirib, B., Rubel-Lifschitzd, T., and Nadlera, A. "The tendency for interpersonal victimhood: The personality construct and its consequences." *Personality and Individual Differences* 165 (2020) 11013. https://www.gwern.net/docs/psychology/personality/2020-gabay.pdf

Hadsall and Associates. Created 2001, revised 2010. "Characteristics of Sexually Healthy Adults." https://www.health.state.mn.us/people/sexualhealth/characteristics.pdf

Hanson, R. K., & Bussière, M. T. (1998). "Predicting relapse: A meta-analysis of sexual offender recidivism studies." *Journal of Consulting and Clinical Psychology*, 66(2), 348–362. https://doi.org/10.1037/0022-006X.66.2.348

Jersey Psychology and Wellbeing Service. May 2020. "The Window of Tolerance: Supporting the wellbeing of children and young people. (Information and ideas for families and schools reconnecting after lockdown.)" https://www.gov.je/SiteCollectionDocuments/Education/ID The Window of Tolerance 20 06 16.pdf

Lane AS, Roberts C. Contextualised reflective competence: a new learning model promoting reflective practice for clinical training. BMC Med Educ. 2022 Jan 30;22(1):71. doi: 10.1186/s12909-022-03112-4. PMID: 35093060; PMCID: PMC8801113.

Martens, T., Daily, B., Hodgson, M. *Characteristics and Dynamics of Incest and Child Sexual Abuse*. Nechi Institute on Alcohol and Drug Education (1988).

Restorative Justice Exchange website. http://restorativejustice.org/#sthash.ctE2wziC.dpbs

Sebben, Cody R. *Brief Communication: Public Perception of Sexual Assault - A Comparison. Sexual Offender Treatment*, Volume 6 (2011), Issue 2. http://sexual-offender-treatment.org/101.html

Simons, D.A. https://smart.ojp.gov/somapi/chapter-3-sex-offender-typologies#pedophilic-and-nonpedophilic-distinction

Wood, Julie T. *Gendered Lives: Communication, Gender and Culture*. Cengage Learning (1994).

http://www.powerandcontrolfilm.com

https://www.mind.org.uk/information-support/types-of-mental-health-problems/dissociation-and-dissociative-disorders/about-dissociation/

Resources

The book which started my healing journey was a controversial and polarizing self-help book *The Courage to Heal: A Guide for Women Survivors of Child Sexual Abuse* written by Ellen Bass and Laura Davis. Their courage to put into writing what survivors of sexual abuse experience left me knowing for the first time I was not alone. There is a life beyond the experiences which cause you to suffer. I hope this book and the resources I share help you know you're not alone and help you return to wholeness.

The most powerful process I use with all my clients that helps them transform their false beliefs is True You Awakening created by Katherine Woodward Thomas, New York Times bestselling author of the book, *Conscious Uncoupling*. I also use Katherine's Inner Sanctuary of Safety, which bridges the gap between our young and current self.

Sexual abuse lives in the body. Survivors of childhood sexual abuse tend to dissociate from their bodies, but true healing comes from fully inhabiting the body. Body oriented therapy models guide clients into their bodies at a pace which is safe and manageable. As a graduate of Hakomi, a somatic psychotherapy, I highly recommend this model.

Knowing how to clearly communicate feelings and needs increases safety in relationships. Nonviolent Communication developed by Marshall Rosenberg is a communication model which contributes to taking responsibility and understanding between people.

Knowing how to talk to children about their bodies and their sexuality significantly increases their safety. Knowing how to guide a child who has been sexually abused can positively impact their choices later in life. Here is a fact sheet and some valuable research:

- https://www.nctsn.org/sites/default/files/resources/fact-sheet/caring_for_kids_what_parents_need_know_about_sexual_abuse.pdf
- https://saccwindsor.net/wp-content/uploads/2020/04/Childrens-sexual-behaviour.pdf

These two books should be read by every person who has been abused or has children to learn how to help and guide children.

- *Understanding Children's Sexual Behaviors: What's Natural and Healthy* by Toni Cavanagh Johnson, PhD
- *Helping Children with Sexual Behavior Problems: A Guidebook for Professionals and Caregivers* by Toni Cavanagh Johnson, PhD

The article referred to in Part Six regarding roles of family members by Sabrina Trobak should be read by anyone experiencing sexual abuse within a family.

https://www.theravive.com/research/families-of-sexual-abuse%3A-the-roles-each-member-plays

Here are some valuable books to support your healing:

- *Born to Win* by Muriel James and Dorothy Jongeward
- *Games People Play* by Eric Berne
- *Healing the Child Within* by Charles Whitfield
- *Homecoming* by John Bradshaw
- *I'm Okay You're Okay* by Thomas Harris
- *Inner Bonding* by Margaret Paul
- *The Inner Child Workbook* by Cathryn Taylor
- *Reconciliation* by Thich Nhat Hanh
- *Recovery of your Inner Child* by Lucia Capacchione
- *Scripts People Live* by Claude Steiner
- *The Tapping Solution* by Nick Ortner

To find a more extensive list of resources, please visit: leilareyes.com/freedomfromshame

About the Author

From the depths of childhood trauma to the joy of personal freedom, Leila Reyes embodies the transformative power of resilience, self-discovery, and liberation. Her experience has ignited a passionate mission to illuminate the path for others toward a life of happiness, fulfillment, and authentic self-expression.

Armed with a master's degree in social work and specialized training in Hakomi, a cutting-edge somatic psychotherapy, Leila has honed her skills as a beacon of transformation. As the lead coach for Your Year of Miracles, created by Marci Shimoff, with certifications in Spiritual Divorce and The Best Year of Your Life by Debbie Ford, and specializing in Katherine Woodward Thomas' True You Awakening, Leila's expertise is unparalleled. She has mastered the art of guiding individuals through the dark tunnels of their trauma-induced beliefs toward the light of their true potential.

Leila's journey is characterized by deep, transformative work, guiding clients through the quagmire of trauma-induced beliefs to reclaim their inherent wholeness. She guides her clients to forge deep connections with themselves, fostering an integration of their internal and external expressions revealing their true selves. Her clients emerge from their journey equipped to free themselves from the impact of trauma and create the enriching quality relationships and lives they long for. Leila's contribution to her clients' growth reflects her unwavering commitment to unveiling the true potential inside each person she guides.

The Freedom Project

Part of my mission is to encourage people to speak out about their experience with childhood sexual abuse. It's through our stories and open conversations that we can heal as individuals, families, and communities.

Have you been affected by childhood sexual abuse and are you ready to talk about it? Please consider visiting my website to learn how to share your story and participate in The Freedom Project.

I want to hear from you if:

- You were sexually abused as a child or adolescent.
- You sexually abused someone and want to learn how to take responsibility and make amends.
- You love someone who has been impacted by childhood sexual abuse and are impacted by their experience.

You're welcome to share your story anonymously if that feels safer to you.

Visit leilareyes.com/freedomfromshame and click The Freedom Project.

For more great books from Empower Press
Visit Books.GracePointPublishing.com

If you enjoyed reading *Freedom from Shame* and purchased it through an online retailer, please return to the site and write a review to help others find the book.

www.ingramcontent.com/pod-product-compliance
Lightning Source LLC
Chambersburg PA
CBHW081847170426
43199CB00018B/2835